A

ROCK-CLIMBING GUIDES
TO THE
ENGLISH LAKE DISTRICT

EDITED BY H. M. KELLY

GREAT
LANGDALE

SECOND SERIES

GREAT LANGDALE

BY WILLIAM CLEGG,
A. R. DOLPHIN & J. W. COOK
WITH ILLUSTRATIONS
BY W. HEATON COOPER

PUBLISHED BY THE FELL & ROCK CLIMBING
CLUB OF THE ENGLISH LAKE DISTRICT

George Basterfield's Edition Published 1926

William Clegg's Edition 1938

Present Edition 1950

Printed by The Cloister Press Ltd.,
Heaton Mersey, Stockport

CONTENTS

EDITOR'S NOTE

This Volume, the third of a New Series of Rock-Climbing Guides in process of publication by the Fell & Rock Climbing Club, is confined to Great Langdale. In the last series, because of the small number of climbs in the area, Great Langdale shared a volume with Dow Crag.

At that time, the low-lying, somewhat short crags which abound in the Langdale Valley were by-passed for others in higher and remoter regions. The possibilities of Langdale were not fully appreciated until the war years (1939-45) when because of consequent restrictions on leisure and travelling its relatively easy accessibility proved to be a godsend to rock-starved climbers. Their concentration on this area gave a fillip to exploration which gathered momentum in succeeding years. This activity, which resulted in the discovery of a galaxy of new climbs, continued to the time of going to press and accounts for the description of the Girdle Traverse of Pavey Ark being by way of Appendix.

Great Langdale now offers an abundance of climbs of a variety and standard equal to those of other climbing grounds in the Lake District ; well equipped with climbing huts and hostels, and a road right into its heart, this valley is likely to become the most popular of all—in fact, the Ogwen Valley of the Lake District !

The possibility of this Guide being the largest in the series should give some idea of the task undertaken by the Authors—particularly Dolphin and Cook. The opening of new crags too, has necessitated extra illustrations by Heaton Cooper. The following pages indicate how efficiently their work has been done, and all users of the Guide will assuredly be grateful to them.

September, 1950.

GENERAL NOTE

Attention is drawn to the following points :—

The grading of the climbs in difficulty refers to ascents, and to dry weather conditions, and follows, in the main, the traditional classification originally introduced by O. G. Jones.

Footgear. All the climbs below the severe standard can be done in nailed boots. While boots are also practicable for many of the severes and very severes, most climbers prefer to use rubbers, or similar footgear, for these climbs. In some cases the use of boots is definitely to be deprecated owing to the danger of wearing away the holds. Whilst not wishing in any way to prescribe the tactics to be adopted, we have ventured to offer suggestions under this head with regard to particular climbs in cases where we feel that it may be helpful.

The pitches have been described in the simplest terms, and any attempt to interfere with the climber's own technique in the art has been avoided as much as possible.

The amount of rope given as required by the leader is net, i.e., the length between him and the second man, leaving out of account waist length. The leader is further advised not to stint himself of rope, especially on the more severe climbs. The length given for each pitch is to the nearest five feet, and is not always the actual height between start and finish, but indicates the length of climbing involved. The same applies to the total lengths of climbs as given.

Except where specially mentioned the climbs are suitable for a party of any number.

The terms ' left ' and ' right,' unless otherwise stated, mean as the climber is facing his climb.

The angle of a glacis is such that it can be walked up ; a slab is steeper ; whilst a wall is nearly vertical and may overhang. The slopes are approximately : below 30°, between 30° and 75°, above 75°.

PREFATORY NOTE

This Guide to Great Langdale is largely based on the last one for the district. Our survey of this area prompted few alterations to Clegg's work and we have been glad to incorporate most of it in substance together with his excellent historical review. As William Clegg is, in effect, a collaborator in the present Guide, his name is included as joint author.

We are grateful to those who have helped with the checking of routes, both old and new, especially to D. C. Birch and J. Bloor, while the friendly advice of many others has always been of material assistance. Our thanks are likewise due to W. Heaton Cooper for his incomparable diagrams.

We regret that it has not been possible to bring all the illustrations up to date ; we trust, however, that the description of the climbs in the text may be sufficiently clear to make up for any omissions therein. Finally, we ask forbearance if the arrangement if the somewhat cumbersome Classified List does not suit all tastes.

J.W.C., A.R.D., 16 April, 1950

HISTORICAL

The history of any one climbing ground can never be regarded as a complete story in itself. Rather is it but one ingredient in the history of a whole district's climbing. Where, in the early days, a new climb, or even a new type of climb, was discovered on any one crag, that in itself showed the way to similar routes on other crags, or even to the exploitation of new crags where this newer type of climb was waiting to be led. And so the histories of all crags become but one all-embracing story. Nowhere has this been better demonstrated than in that excellent article by H. M. Kelly and J. H. Doughty in the *Fell and Rock Climbing Club Journal* of 1936. There it is shown how the original story of English rock-climbing is a story of summit seeking—of easy-way finding.

Langdale offered no such summits, no such easy-ways. Langdale crags, Gimmer and Bowfell in particular, had their impressiveness—not one of broken, towering massiveness such as the Pillar and Scafell—but one of vast, airy smoothness, in no way inviting to the early pioneers. Little, too, was to be seen of the comfort of chimney and crack, beloved of the second group of our early climbers. But what little there was of this was duly noted by W. P. Haskett-Smith, most aptly named ' the prince of pioneers.' So in the 1880's he climbed the North-west Gully on Gimmer, the two Pavey Ark Gullies, and the North Gully of Bowfell Buttress. This was the real start of rock-climbing in Langdale, though Jack's Rake, probably known to shepherds from very early times, had been crossed within the previous decade by R. Pendlebury.

Perhaps, therefore, it would be unfair to say that Langdale lagged behind the other centres in its climbing history although its first ascents came half-a-century later. More fairly one might say that Langdale took its true position in the story of English climbing, starting at the beginning of the ' Gully Epoch.' The remainder of the century completed this with the addition of the two Pavey Ark chimneys and a few outlying scrambles on Bowfell.

It was with the ' Slab and Wall ' period that Langdale came into its own. The Langdale crags, Gimmer in particular, are perfect examples of this type. So, in the first decade of this century, the first climbs typical of Langdale began. H. B. Lyon and E. Rigby started the Gimmer alphabet. Bowfell Buttress climb and the Crescent on Pavey Ark opened up the two other main crags. From that time until the war, development in Langdale, though much of it was on outlying minor crags, went steadily ahead.

During the war activity ceased.

Then came the great boom period, and in addition to his exploits on other crags, G. S. Bower quickly added a round half-dozen routes in this area. His ascents of ' D ' on Gimmer and Crescent Slabs on Pavey Ark advanced Langdale climbing by almost one full stage in severity. H. B. Lyon returned, seventeen years after his original ascents of ' B ' and Lyon's Crawl, to add Bracket and Slab Climb, Chimney Buttress, and White Gill Chimney to the list. In 1924 the first of the ' very-severes ' came from J. A. Wray with ' E ' route, and M. de Selincourt, in addition to four new routes (climbed solo), added the second with his ascent of the Right-Hand Wall of Bowfell.

Two years later G. S. Bower again looked round the North-west Side of Gimmer, which he had opened out in 1920 with Ash-tree Slabs, and added Pallid Slabs and Hiatus. Then in their ' laudable attempt ' to put G. Basterfield's newly published Langdale Guide quickly out of date, A. B. Reynolds, H. S. Gross, and G. G. Macphee added another three ' very severes ' on this side. Reynolds' final ascent of the Crack was the culmination of a very determined siege of a most noteworthy route. So came into being what, for a short time, was known as the ' Gentlemen's Side ' of Gimmer, in comparison with the easier and now much be-touristed routes on the other faces. But not for long did the North-west Face merit this title, for Miss N. Ridyard quickly had them all ticked off.

By now Gimmer had a veritable network of routes on all its faces—there seemed little room for more—though never let it be said that there *is* no room. However, subsequent exploration has been concerned mostly with other crags. In addition to routes on minor crags, four new routes have been added on the Bowfell crags, and two ' very-severes,' Deer Bield Crack in Far Easedale, and Stoats' Crack on Pavey Ark, have added greatly to the quality and prestige of Langdale climbing. The girdling of Gimmer has also been completed.

Today rock-climbing enjoys more popularity than ever before. The number of its devotees has grown enormously in recent years, and Langdale—so easily accessible from the civilized part of the Lake District, therefore becomes perhaps *the* most popular playground for the sport. What new climbs will this great influx of climbers add to our sport—what new methods—what new developments ? The next new guide to rock-climbing in Langdale shall tell.

WM. CLEGG, 1938

HISTORICAL (1938-49)

Langdale remains as popular a centre as ever, as witness the fact that the number of recorded climbs in the area has been more than doubled since the publication of the last Guide. Even during the war years activity was considerable, many finding the fells and crags ideally suited for precious leaves away from front-line England. Throughout this time the name of R. J. Birkett has figured prominently. His ascent of ' F ' Route was probably the most notable achievement at a time when Gimmer still offered tantalising possibilities along natural weaknesses. Sydney Thompson and John Ashton, also contributed several fine routes here, but by the early 1940's interest almost inevitably began to be directed towards the further exploration of other crags. On Bowfell, the Buttress was ' girdled ' but otherwise produced little of real merit. Pavey Ark was rescued from its rather traditional status of a purely wet-weather cliff by the discovery of a number of good buttress climbs of all grades of difficulty, culminating in H. A. Carsten's magnificent Rake End Wall.

Despite this progress on the major crags, undoubtedly the most important feature of recent exploration in Langdale has been the development of White Ghyll and, to a lesser degree, of Raven Crag. The former had already provided routes of quality in its classic Chimney and Slab climbs, but it was J. W. Haggas's epic ascent of the Gordian Knot which revealed the possibilities of the previously untouched, but extremely imposing, central mass. Five years elapsed before Birkett made the second ascent of this fine climb and then went on to pioneer a host of worthy routes along the entire range of the Crag, of which Haste Not and Perhaps Not rank among the best and hardest climbs in the district. The opening-out of Raven Crag was due in the main to the industry of A. Gregory,

though Bilberry Buttress, perhaps the most attractive route
ere, was climbed quite early in the period by C. F. Rolland.
The network of climbs now to be found on this crag is
dequately justified by its extreme accessibility.

Among this spate of novelties the older routes have lost little
of their warranted reputation. Established favourites, such as
Gimmer Crack, may seem a trifle easier now that the trail is
well blazoned ; Right-Hand Wall has shed most of its legendary
rmour. The intrinsic difficulties of Deer Bield Crack,
however, are as acute as ever, even if the most formidable
problem in the district today is Kipling Groove.

In concluding his Historical note in 1938, Clegg pondered
on the future of the sport in Great Langdale. Today the
general standard of climbing is undoubtedly higher. New
methods too (such as the carrying of pitons for use in emergency
and a more scientific system of rope handling and belaying)
have been introduced as safety measures, though they cannot
be said directly to have influenced the recent exploration of the
district. Future climbers will no doubt have their own story
of further developments.

J.W.C., A.R.D., 1950

GIMMER CRAG

THE APPROACHES

GREAT LANGDALE.—The New and Old Hotels are the usual starting points.

From behind the New Hotel the ordinary Langdale Pikes track leads on to the fellside, turns left over a small wooden bridge and rises up the steep grass bank running north-west above the left bank of Dungeon Ghyll. After a few hundred feet, the track zigzags over steeper ground to arrive at a large undulating plateau, with Harrison Stickle rising ahead. The track, now almost level, is still followed to the left, but, when it begins to rise again steeply to the col above where Gimmer Crag comes in sight, it is forsaken for an indefinite level track which keeps left over a subsidiary ridge and leads over the scree in a few hundred yards to the foot of South-east Gully.

From the back of the Old Hotel, the route starts up a grassy bank with fell walls on either side, turns behind the wall on the left, crosses the scree and rises, zigzagging generally in a north-westerly direction. It then keeps fairly low to avoid the deeper gullies and steeper outcrops hereabouts. Gimmer Crag, though, is soon sighted above and the track rises gradually, passing below what is in summer a very welcome little waterfall, crosses the scree and reaches again the foot of South-east Gully.

The ascent of Middlefell Buttress (q.v.), or the gully on its left, is a third common method of approach to Gimmer Crag. From the top of either of these a steep direct ascent of the fellside soon leads to the Pikes' track coming up from the New Hotel, and this is followed as before.

BORROWDALE.—The obvious route is to follow Stake Pass up Langstrath and turn left at the top across the moor running up to Pike o' Stickle, and continue on to arrive at the top of Gimmer Crag.

TOPOGRAPHICAL

Gimmer Crag, though not a Pike itself, is from the rock-climbing point of view, the central attraction of the justly famous Langdale Pikes.

Seen from across the valley the crag breaks out from the scree abruptly, almost from a single point, and rises in a gradually widening (but broken) incline, for some two hundred and fifty feet to its point of greatest width, where its form changes. Here comes a series of rounded grassy terraces. The crag's broken nature ends. It steepens and rises as a smooth, rather conical pillar for two hundred feet to a rounded top lying against the fellside.

Being but a single buttress, unmarred by gullies, its topography is simple. In general, it faces south-west but on closer inspection the rough conical shape of its upper section divides itself into three main Faces, namely, the North-west, the West, and the South-east. The North-west and the South-east Faces sweep down into the two similarly named embracing gullies which hold Gimmer Crag aloof from the general fellside. The West Face abuts on the rounded terraces forming the top of the lower broken section.

South-east Gully and Junipall Gully, situated on opposite sides of the crag, are evidence of a fault which just fails to isolate Gimmer Crag from the main mountain. Junipall

Gully runs steeply down and at right angles into the North
west Gully.

The wall above Junipall Gully is known as Pallid Buttress
while the bounding wall to the South-east Gully is called
Main Wall.

Approaching by the track from Great Langdale the silhouette
of the steep West Face and the frontal view of the smooth
South-west Face form a memorable picture. One arrives at
the foot of South-east Gully and, fortunately, above the broken
lower sweep of the crag. The South-east Face climbs are
immediately at hand. Ahead lies the Bilberry Chute, the eastern
end of one of the lower of our rounded terraces. An obvious
scrambling zigzag track leads up to it and from terrace to
terrace until the highest, Ash-tree Ledge, is reached. Here
starts the network of the West Face climbs.

The North-west Face, with its cracks and overhangs so
different from the other Faces, is reached with slightly more
trouble and in a variety of ways. From the foot of the Bilberry
Chute one can walk down alongside the buttress, round its
toe, and up the steep grass in the lower part of North-west
Gully. Alternatively, from about midway between the Bilberry Chute and Ash-tree Ledge, one obvious terrace entirely
crosses the face, until a vertical twenty-five foot descent of some
difficulty, where a rope may be of service, lands one at the foot
of Ash-tree Slabs. The third method adopted for reaching this
Face is the actual descent of Ash-tree Slabs from Ash-tree
Ledge, which of course requires rope and the necessary skill.
The North-west Face differs again from the other two main
Faces in that, while all their climbs lead to the summit (with
the exception of Prelude), this Face continues along the lower
broken part of the crag, and the climbs on that section lead
only to Ash-tree Ledge.

For descent after a climb, the South-east Gully will be found almost level with the top of the West Face and just a few yards away to the right. The usual method is to enter from the left and continue on this side until about half-way down, then crossing and finishing by the right side (looking in). A certain amount of care is needed on loose scree and one short scoop. This lands one again at the foot of the Bilberry Chute.

Junipall Gully leads conveniently from the top to the north-west side. It will be found by wandering up several terraces to the left from the top of the West Face. This Gully, too, requires a little care—it is usually rather muddy for rubbers.

A direct descent to Ash-tree Ledge by one of the easier West Face climbs may involve some congestion with ascending parties.

The climbs on Pallid Buttress are readily accessible from the North-west Gully.

The Climbs

MAIN WALL CLIMB.—160 feet. Very difficult. This climb runs up the steep, but broken, face which forms the right-hand bounding wall of South-east Gully. An almost infinite variety of routes can be found on it but the most continuous and obvious, as here described, is the direct route up the cleanest part, the right-hand edge. Starts at an embedded rock at the foot of the wall a little below the obvious large detached flake.

(1) 55 feet. Climb straight up the steep wall on good holds to a bilberry ledge with an assortment of small belays.

(2) 30 feet. A diagonal traverse to the left leads to an obvious stance.

(3) 35 feet. Step right and proceed directly up again to a good belay.

(4) 40 feet. Start slightly left and then continue up, finishing by a pull-out on the left of a large loose block, or by a scoop on its right.

South-east Face

South-east Gully.—Only an easy scramble, providing a useful means of descent from the summit to the climbs on the South-east Face, or to the foot of the Bilberry Chute. (See Topographical.)

Bachelor Crack.—175 feet. Very severe. Follows the right-hand edge of the South-east Face overlooking the Gully. Although considerably exposed towards the top the main difficulty is in the second pitch. Starts from the South-east Gully at the highest accessible point on the left wall at a crack in a corner.

(1) 20 feet. The corner is climbed by means of holds in the crack and on the left wall to a small grass ledge, which is attained by an awkward movement. Junction with Chimney Buttress, which goes up to the left. Small spike-belay above, suitable only for line.

(2) 35 feet. Chimney Buttress is followed for about six feet to surmount the bulge. A delicate traverse to the right is then made, crossing the crack on sloping holds, to the rib overlooking the Gully. A few feet higher is a small grass ledge with a flake-belay on the right.

(3) 30 feet. The wall above is climbed on the right, on good holds, to a bilberry ledge. Belay.

(4) 45 feet. Up to another bilberry ledge. Flake-belay on wall.

(5)   45 feet. The rib ahead is followed by easy ledges to the top.

CHIMNEY BUTTRESS.—210 feet. Severe. Chief interest is in the long second pitch. Commences in South-east Gully a few feet below the start of Bachelor Crack.

(1)   40 feet. A 6-foot crack followed by scrambling over grass ledges leading upwards and to the left.

(2)   90 feet. From a point on a large ledge, a few feet to the right of Gimmer Chimney, climb diagonally up to the right to a big block near the edge of South-east Gully. (Junction with Bachelor Crack.) From the block ascend the steep wall above, over the ' piano pitch,' and continue up slabs to a good bilberry ledge.

(3)   80 feet. The pleasant slabs above.

GIMMER CHIMNEY.—260 feet. Very difficult. Obvious twin cracks, running practically the full length of the South-east Face mark a very satisfying wet-day climb. Starts at a cairn some 20 feet above and to the right of the Bracket and Slab Climb.

(1)   45 feet. Climb the broken rib to a stance and belays.

(2)   25 feet. An easy chimney is followed to a grass ledge with a good belay on the floor immediately below the next steep bit.

(3)   30 feet. After an awkward start, easy rocks lead to a good stance on the right.
     Pitches 2 and 3 are usually combined.

(4)   25 feet. Traverse left for 10 feet into a difficult groove which leads to a sentry box fitted with a juniper bush.

(5)   30 feet. Climb the deep crack above, via large holds on its right rib, to a stance at the right-hand end of the Gangway.

(6)   35 feet. The chimney above is the sixth pitch of the
        Bracket and Slab Climb. Walk 15 feet to the right
        and climb the easier chimney there to the open gully
        above with a belay on the right wall.
(7)   70 feet. This pitch leads, first by the gully bed, then by
        the right rib, with a step left, to the summit.

BRACKET AND SLAB CLIMB.—295 feet. Severe. (Barely so if
        Pitch 6 is avoided.) A varied climb of an unusual
        length for Gimmer Crag. Starts to the right of the
        buttress at a pointed rock flake some 20 feet above the
        level of the point at which the path from Langdale
        reaches the crag.
(1)   35 feet. Climb over the tip of the flake to a grass ledge,
        thence over an awkward slab to a bilberry ledge. The
        right wall forms a belay.
(2)   65 feet. Move a few feet rightwards to the rib which
        leads in 35 feet on to a further grassy bank. This is
        followed to a belay in the rocky corner at the top.
(3)   40 feet. The Bracket. A horizontal traverse to the right for
        20 feet over good blocks is followed by a difficult groove.
(4)   40 feet. Traverse diagonally right over easy rocks to a
        line belay at the foot of the Neat Bit, passing Amen
        Corner on the left.
(5)   25 feet. The Neat Bit. Follow the ledge running diag-
        onally left for 15 feet, then up the crack to the Gang-
        way. Belay on left at top of Amen Corner.
        Walk 20 feet right to the foot of the first of two chimneys.
        Line-belay at its foot.
(6)   25 feet. The strenuous chimney. If desired it can be
        avoided by the easier chimney on the right. Both

arrive at the same place where a good flake-belay exists high on the right wall.

(7) 30 feet. The left wall is climbed, working leftwards over pleasant slabs to a good ledge and belay.

(8) 35 feet. Move right to the edge of Gimmer Chimney and then straight up slabs to the top.

SOUTH-EAST LOWER TRAVERSE.—95 feet. Difficult. Starts at a little cave some 50 feet above the foot of the South-east Gully. Serves as a short cut from the Gully to the West Face—or as a useful means of descent.

(1) 55 feet. From the small cave follow a fault running upwards to the left to a small sentry box. Alternatively, starting 15 feet below the cave, a pleasant wall followed by a scoop leads in 50 feet to the belay in Gimmer Chimney below pitch 4 ; the Chimney then leads to the sentry box.

(2) 40 feet. Climb out over the left wall and traverse left to the foot of Amen Corner.

A higher and easier traverse leads from the start of Chimney Buttress across Gimmer Chimney, then via the slabs to the Gangway at the top of Amen Corner.

THE WEST FACE

PRELUDE.—245 feet. Difficult. An uninteresting route on the broken rocks below Ash-tree Ledge. Difficulties can usually be avoided as many variations are possible. Starts at the lowest point of the Buttress at a small ash-tree below a sweep of slabs.

(1) 45 feet. Climb the slab, passing a block, to a grassy corner with good spike-belay on left.

(2) 65 feet. Step round to the left and up to a groove about

20 feet away. This is followed by easy rocks to the foot of a rib. Belay.

(3)   55 feet. The rib is followed by easy scrambling to a large flake-belay.

(4)   80 feet. A short slab, a traverse left, and another slab give on to easy ground leading to the main highway.

CROW'S NEST DIRECT.—210 feet. Very severe. Though rather artificial, provides interesting climbing. Starts at the lower right-hand end of Ash-tree Ledge at a small ash-tree. The Bracket, on Bracket and Slab Climb, is 20 feet above on the right.

(1)   15 feet. The narrow crack in the corner leads easily to a small belay.

(2)   30 feet. The steep, open groove above the belay and on the left of the corner is entered with extreme difficulty and followed to a belay at the back of a grass ledge.

(3)   30 feet. A small pedestal at the rear of the ledge provides a useful take-off for the ascent of the bulging wall above. A narrow crack is reached 15 feet to the left of Amen Corner. Belay.

(4)   25 feet. The crack is climbed by the layback method. (Pitch 1, Musgrave's Traverse.) It leads to the Gangway which is followed up to the left to a small belay below an overhang.

(5)   60 feet. A sensational upward hand-traverse is made on good holds across the overhang to the right until a pull-over can be made onto a small ledge above the overhang. The rocks above lead leftwards to the arête on the right of Green Chimney which is followed to the Crow's Nest. Belay on right.

(6)   50 feet.   Step out to the left and climb the corner immediately above, when easy slabs lead to the summit.

VARIATION START—GREEN GAMBIT.—Provides an alternative to the rather excessive groove of Pitch 2 without
depriving the climb of its interest.   Commences 25
feet to the left of the original start.

(1)   15 feet.   Easy rocks to good belay below a green, overhanging groove.

(2)   30 feet.   The groove above is climbed, the exit proving
rather awkward.   The grass shelf at the top of the
second pitch of the ordinary route is then reached.

' B ' ROUTE.—180 feet.   Severe in boots.   Perhaps the most
popular route on the Crag.   Starts 15 feet to the left
of the large cairn on Ash-tree Ledge.

(1)   30 feet.   Up to the large platform on the right.

(2)   15 feet.   25 feet to the right is an open crack with a block
at its foot.   This leads to Thomson's Ledge.

(3)   15 feet.   Amen Corner.   The obvious layback crack 20
feet to the right.   One lands on the Gangway with an
excellent belay on the floor to the left.

(4)   30 feet.   Ascend the Gangway to the left to a good ledge
and belay.

(5)   40 feet.   The Green Chimney immediately above is
climbed until a short traverse to the right gives access
to a comfortable ledge, the Crow's Nest, just round
the corner.   Small belays on the right.

(6)   50 feet.   Step to the right out of the Nest and follow
pleasant slabs to the top.

' C ' ROUTE.—170 feet.   Severe.   Takes a natural and pleasing
line straight up the Face.   The first pitch is shared

with ' A ' and ' B ' Routes.   From the large platform
thus attained pitch 2 lies up the steep wall, 10 feet left
of ' A ' and ' B.'

(2)   15 feet.   The scoop on the right leads to Thomson's
Ledge.   The only belay is a small one in a little
hollow 10 feet to the right.

(3)   35 feet.   The steep groove immediately above may be
started direct or in a little chimney on the left.   Neither
way is easy.   Follow the groove and step over the
right wall at the top to the stance and belay at the foot
of Green Chimney.

(4)   35 feet.   Step back to the left and climb diagonally left
across Lyon's Crawl to a small belay below a prominent
flat overhang.

(5)   55 feet.   Climb up to the overhang where good holds are
found for the pull-out to the left.   Continue up a
groove to a good ledge, then bear right up the depression in the face above to the finishing balcony.

' A ' ROUTE.—220 feet.   Severe in boots.   A series of steps
rising to the left.   The first two pitches as far as
Thomson's Ledge are identical with those of ' B '
Route.

(3)   30 feet.   Traverse left along Thomson's Ledge to the
foot of Forty-Foot Corner.   A flat-topped spike on the
left affords a poorish belay for line only ; a better one
can be obtained by climbing 20 feet up the Corner.

(4)   40 feet.   The Corner is climbed to a good spike-belay at
the top.

(5)   20 feet.   Traverse left and slightly upwards to a ledge
and large belay immediately beneath an open groove,
Lichen Chimney.

(6)   35 feet. Lichen Chimney. Good flake-belay on the
        wall 6 feet above and to the left of the finish.

(7)   25 feet. The rock staircase on the left leads to a corner
        below a crack. Spike-belays on the left.

(8)   20 feet. A steep crack with good holds.

DIPHTHONG.—170 feet. Very severe. Originally a direct start
        to the upper half of ' E ' Route ; it now possesses an
        independent finish. The technical difficulty of its
        second pitch is perhaps the climb's main *raison d'être*.

(1)—   The first pitch is in common with ' A,' ' B ' and ' C '
        Routes (q.v.). From the large platform the next
        pitch attacks the wall above at its steepest accessible
        point, some 10 feet left of ' C, ' and immediately
        beneath Forty-foot Corner.

(2)   30 feet. A series of three overhanging steps leads to
        Thomson's Ledge. The greatest difficulty is in
        surmounting the first of these. Horizontal flake-belay
        at the foot of Forty-foot Corner.

(3)   35 feet. The steep ridge on the immediate right of
        Forty-foot Corner is climbed on small holds until,
        after 10 feet, improved holds lead rather to the right.
        The belay at the foot of Green Chimney can be used
        by stepping over the wall to the right.

(4)   75 feet. Step back to the left and across to Lyon's Crawl,
        then straight up to the right of ' C ' Overhang and
        towards the upper part of Green Chimney. The
        Chimney is avoided as far as possible, the finish being
        up a steep, indefinite arête just to the right of ' C.'

OLIVERSON'S VARIATION AND LYON'S CRAWL.—170 feet. Very
        difficult. Follows the easiest line up this part of the

Crag. Starts from Ash-tree Ledge 15 feet to the left of the start of ' A.' and ' B ' Routes.

(1) 20 feet. Moderate climbing direct to a good belay.

(2) 30 feet. Traverse horizontally right on good holds for 15 feet and then directly up to a small stance halfway up the left edge of Forty-foot Corner. Two small belays above.

(3) 20 feet. Climb directly over the belays and follow the left edge to the top of Forty-foot Corner. Belay on floor.

(4) 20 feet. Start of Lyon's Crawl. Traverse upwards and to the right, using an obvious crack for the hands, to a large belay.

(5) 30 feet. Continue up to the right into Green Chimney and thence across the right wall into the Crow's Nest.

(6) 50 feet. Step right and up the slabs to the top (final pitch of ' B ').

' E ' ROUTE.—210 feet. Severe. Delicate and somewhat exposed. Originally a variation start to ' A ' Route— later continued throughout as a separate climb. Starts at the same point as ' A,' ' B ' and ' C.'

(1) 40 feet. After 15 feet of easy climbing from Ash-tree Ledge turn left up a sort of cave pitch. Easy rocks on the left lead to the belay at the top of the first pitch of Oliverson's Variation.

(2) 55 feet. Traverse the flaky wall diagonally left for 40 feet to a ledge and across to a crack with a small but good belay on its right rib.

(3) 30 feet. The crack is climbed for about 15 feet when a delicate traverse leads out to the right to the belay at the foot of Lichen Chimney.

4) 25 feet. Continue the traverse upwards to the right, crossing the arête to reach the small belays below the cave on ' C.'

5) 60 feet. An airy pitch on satisfying holds. Step back left into the groove on the arête and climb straight up past the ledge which runs from ' C ' to the top of Lichen Chimney. Continue up the blunt nose of the buttress to the finishing balcony, landing midway between the finishes of ' A ' and ' C. '

LICHEN GROOVE.—160 feet. Severe. Follows a direct line up the face by way of the shallow groove which becomes most pronounced in Lichen Chimney. The second pitch is the hardest. Starts just to the left of ' A ' and ' B ' at the foot of a slight nose.

1) 30 feet. Up the nose by a thin crack on its right edge to a junction with Oliverson's Variation at the top of the first pitch.

2) 60 feet. Move up diagonally right for a few feet and make an awkward ascent into a shallow groove. The groove is followed up to the left on small holds to the belays at the foot of Lichen Chimney. (This pitch was originally part of Musgrave's Traverse.)

3) 30 feet. Climb Lichen Chimney or, as in the first ascent, avoid it by climbing an ill-defined groove a few feet to the right. Belay at top of Lichen Chimney.

4) 40 feet. Continue up the corner above (a continuation of Lichen Chimney) on very good holds to finish midway between ' A ' and ' E.'

D ' ROUTE.—100 feet. Severe. A route of character despite its brevity. Starts some 40 feet above Ash-tree Ledge

at a grassy terrace below an overhanging, triangula
recess, reached by scrambling up to the left from
point 20 feet to the left of Oliverson's Variation.

(1)   10 feet.   The groove below the recess is climbed to a
upstanding belay.

(2)   30 feet.   Enter the recess, then leave it by a delicate
traverse to the left. This leads in 15 feet to an easy
groove sloping up to the right which is followed to
comfortable stance and block-belay.

(3)   45 feet.   The Forked Lightning Crack is climbed to the
belays on the left wall of the recess below the fina
crack on ' A.'

(4)   15 feet.   Climb over the belays on to a sloping corner o
the left, when a delicate balance upwards brings
handhold into reach, though not into sight. Step
out on to the finishing balcony.

WHIT'S END.—95 feet. Very severe. A somewhat hybri
route, yet provides both strenuous and delicate
climbing of considerable interest. It is made more
awkward by the abundance of lichen on this part of
the Crag. Starts a few feet left of ' D ' at the foot of
thin crack.

(1)   30 feet.   The crack, which slants to the left, is climbed
largely by the layback method to a horizontal, mossy
ledge. Spike-belay on right. (Junction with Hyphen.

(2)   15 feet.   Ascend obliquely to the left with the aid of a good
flake-hold to a poor stance and small belay beneath the
overhang. (Pitch 2, ' F ' Route.)

(3)   50 feet.   ' F ' is followed for about 10 feet until a narrow
horizontal crack on the right allows a delicate traverse
to be made across the steep slab (spike for running

belay at commencement of traverse). Continue the traverse on small ledges to the right-hand edge of the slab, rising slightly towards the end. An awkward step downwards is then made and ' D ' Route attained halfway up the Forked Lightning Crack. Belay. Finish up ' D.'

' F ' ROUTE.—130 feet. Very severe. A route of considerable character and difficulty following the overhanging crack which runs up the face to the left of ' D.' Starts just to the left of Whit's End below easy grass ledges.

(1) 45 feet. Scramble up the ledges to the left to top of first pitch of Hyphen and follow the latter up to the right to the good spike-belay.

(2) 15 feet. Ascend obliquely to the left with the aid of a good flake hold to a poor stance and small belay beneath the overhang.

(3) 70 feet. Move up right into the crack which is climbed with increasing difficulty using the edge of the crack and small footholds on the right wall. The last few feet are probably best overcome by the layback method. (Running belays at 15 feet and 30 feet.)

KIPLING GROOVE.—175 feet. Very severe. Extreme severity and a high degree of exposure combine to make the route perhaps the most serious undertaking in the district. Takes the easiest line up the steep rocks between ' F ' Route and the Crack. Starts at the foot of Hyphen.

(1) 40 feet. The first pitch of Hyphen is followed to the flake-belay (for line only) on the grass ledge below the large overhangs.

(2) 35 feet. The smooth wall on the left is traversed either by ascending to the overhang and using the broad crack behind it as handhold, or, as in the first ascent, by stepping up a few feet until a line of small flake-holds can be used for a short, but strenuous, hand-traverse. In either case a tiny moss-covered ledge is reached and the traverse continued to the foot of an open chimney. Ascend the chimney for 15 feet to a comfortable recess and good flake-belay on the right wall.

(3) 100 feet. Climb the right-hand side of the chimney using a series of jammed blocks until progress is stopped by the overhang. Pull out to the right onto the corner and ascend a thin crack until more overhangs are reached necessitating a step right to a small foothold. The next move is the crux. A strenuous arm-pull brings a diagonal crack above the overhang within reach, followed by a horizontal crack a little higher to the right. The latter is used first to surmount the overhang and then as a mantelshelf, footholds being almost non-existent. Traverse right to a resting place at the foot of a thin crack. This is climbed, mainly by hand-jamming, to a good ledge when easier climbing leads to the top.

MUSGRAVE'S TRAVERSE.—140 feet. Severe. Of the almost innumerable ways by which the easier right-hand section of the West Face may be traversed this seems to offer the most obvious and direct connection between the end of the South-east Lower Traverse and ' D ' Route. The first pitch as described is a pleasant piece of climbing of considerable difficulty ; there is an easier alternative by way of Amen Corner and the Gangway. Starts from Thomson's Ledge at a crack a few feet left of Amen Corner (the same crack is used in Pitch 3, Crow's Nest Direct).

(1)   55 feet.   The narrow crack is climbed by the layback method to a sloping ledge on the right.   A three-inch ledge now leads upwards to the left for 20 feet to an airy right-angled corner from which a delicate, descending traverse is made into the groove on ' C.'   There is a good incut handhold for the final swing across. Ascend ' C ' a few feet to spike-belays in the groove, or continue to the better stance at the foot of Green Chimney, a short distance higher on the right.

(2)   20 feet.   A delicate traverse leftwards across Diphthong leads to the belay at the top of Forty-foot Corner.

(3)   20 feet.   Follow ' A ' to the foot of Lichen Chimney. (A very artificial alternative is to descend Oliverson's Variation, Pitch 3, when a line of holds leads across into Lichen Groove ; this is followed to the foot of Lichen Chimney.   This was the line originally taken.)

(4)   45 feet.   A delicate, horizontal traverse leads left across the wall to the belay below the Forked Lightning Crack on ' D.'   The finish is either up or down ' D,' or, more appropriately, down Hyphen.

HYPHEN.—90 feet.   Severe.   A pleasant traverse connecting the top of Asterisk (or Samaritan Corner) with ' D ' Route, thus making possible quite a long, continuous climb.   The final step into ' D ' is the only really awkward move and that is well protected.   Starts at the top of Asterisk, 50 feet below the large overhangs on ' F.'

(1) 40 feet. Climb straight up to a small grass ledge beneath the overhang, avoiding a large, loose-looking block just before the landing. Flake-belay for line only.

(2) 50 feet. Traverse diagonally upwards to the right to a narrow, mossy ledge leading to a bulging corner (spike for running belay). A delicate, two-step move is made round the corner to join ' D ' Route a few feet from the belay below the Forked Lightning Crack.

BARRY's TRAVERSE.—75 feet. Very severe. The easiest direct link between Ash-tree Ledge and The Crack and Hiatus. Useful as a continuation of the various West Face traverses. Starts at the extreme left-hand end of Ash-tree Ledge.

(1) 40 feet. Climb leftwards over easy grass and rocks until a short, steep descent to the left leads to a grass ledge on the right wall of the unclimbed section of The Crack. Belays.

(2) 35 feet. Make a delicate descending traverse into the corner when a strenuous pull-up leads to a ledge on the left wall (block for running belay). Follow the ledge without difficulty to the pedestal belay at the top of Pitch 3 of The Crack. The Hiatus mantelshelf is then immediately to the left.

NORTH-WEST FACE (Lower Section)

INTERLUDE.—90 feet. Very Difficult. A short and not particularly outstanding climb. Starts about 40 feet below a huge detached flake in the lower reaches of the North-west Gully and follows the line of an arête.

(1) 40 feet. The wall on the right of the arête is climbed until the arête itself is gained by making a somewhat awkward step to the left. 20 feet of easier slabs lead to a belay.

(2)　50 feet. Slabs are climbed on good holds to the finish about halfway up the Lower Crag.

CARTWHEEL.—70 feet. Very difficult. Follows a line parallel with Interlude on the left-hand side of the arête, starting from a small boulder about 25 feet below the large flake.

(1)　25 feet. Ascend the slightly bulging rock for 10 feet when the angle eases and a right-angled corner is climbed on good holds to a stance with a belay on the right.

(2)　45 feet. Over the bulge in the groove on the left when the angle again eases and a small heather ledge 15 feet higher on the left can be attained without difficulty. Then straight up on good holds to the finishing ledge. Belays.

HERDWICK BUTTRESS.—90 feet. Very difficult. Starts just to the right of the ash-tree at the foot of Ash-tree Slabs. The first pitch, as originally described, followed the slab which was later made use of as the start of Introduction, but as this appears to have fallen into disuse in favour of the easier chimney on its right it is the latter which will be described.

(1)　40 feet. The open chimney on the right is climbed on good holds to a large shelf with a fine belay on the wall at the back. If desired, the climb can be left at this point which affords the quickest means of descent, i.e., from Ash-tree Ledge to the North-west Face.

(2)　50 feet. Climb above the belay, between two large flakes, to a ledge below thin twin cracks. These provide fair

holds and lead to a terrace running across the upper
face. The start of ' D ' Route is almost immediately
above.

This pitch can be varied from the ledge by climbing
a more obvious crack of about equal degree of difficulty some 15 feet to the right.

INTRODUCTION.—75 feet. Severe. Follows the edge of the
steep slab to the left of Herdwick Buttress, the hardest
part being near the top. Starts immediately behind
the ash-tree.

(1)　15 feet. An easy rock staircase to the right leads to a
belay on the corner below the impending wall.

(2)　60 feet. The slab on the right is climbed, keeping as near
as possible to its left-hand edge. Holds become small
after 30 feet (Spike for running belay on left) and a
bulge is surmounted with the aid of good handholds.
Easier climbing then leads to a grass ledge and belay.

ASH-TREE SLABS.—155 feet. Very difficult. The prominent
slab running up to the left from the small ash-tree at
the foot of Introduction.

(1)　50 feet. Move 10 feet up the corner and traverse diagonally left on good holds to the extreme edge. The edge
is then climbed for 10 feet to a good ledge with belay
above on the left.

(2)　55 feet. Climb left to a pleasant platform 10 feet higher
from which a groove leads up to the right (a good belay
exists 15 feet up the groove for large parties wishing
to make use of the platform). The groove becomes less
steep and numerous belays are to be found.

(3)   50 feet.   From here it is possible to walk easily right to
      Ash-tree Ledge 15 feet away.   The climb, however,
      continues up to the left and terminates on a ledge
      midway between Ash-tree Ledge and the foot of ' D '
      Route.

JOAS.—150 feet.   Very severe.   Starts from a grassy platform in
      North-west Gully 20 feet to the left of Ash-tree Slabs
      and follows the nose of the Buttress.   A strenuous but
      rather artificial climb.
(1)   30 feet.   Climb the overhanging groove running upwards
      to the right to a broken terrace.   Belay in Ash-tree
      Slabs on the right.
(2)   40 feet.   From the terrace, climb an overhanging block
      above by the crack on its right to a small recess.   Move
      left on a good flake until, by means of a very long reach
      to the left, a good handhold can be attained for a pull
      over the overhang.   A small ledge is reached but no
      belay.   Continue slightly left via some jammed stones
      until a long step across to the right can be made to a
      thin crack which leads with difficulty to the platform
      on the second pitch of Ash-tree Slabs.   Belay in the
      groove 15 feet above.
(3)   80 feet.   The narrow slab on the left is climbed on small
      holds, a good ledge being attained by means of an
      awkward move.   Climb first up the corner and then the
      arête on right (good holds) to a large terrace and the
      belay above Asterisk.

NORTH-WEST ARÊTE.—135 feet.   Very severe.   Follows the
      line of the arête between Joas and Asterisk.   A feature
      of the climb is the extremely small stances.   Conse-

quently most suitable for two climbers only who can
apply the tactics of alternate leads. Starts a few
feet to the right of Asterisk below a large overhang.

(1)   25 feet. Climb the wall and traverse right to a very small
      stance and belay about 15 feet below the overhang.

(2)   45 feet. The overhang is turned by means of an awkward
      groove up, and to the left, from the belay. Traverse
      right immediately above the overhang to enter a
      groove on the right of the arête. Small belay and poor
      stance.

(3)   30 feet. The arête is climbed direct on small holds to
      another very small stance and thread-belay below a
      thin, shattered crack. The final section of Asterisk is
      just round to the left.

(4)   35 feet. Finish up the arête, using the thin crack. It
      forms the right-hand side of a partially detached flake
      and should be treated with care.

Asterisk.—125 feet. Very severe. A popular climb up the
      steep wall on the left of North-west Arête. Holds are
      excellent except on the last pitch. Starts to the right
      of the large jammed boulder in the bed of the Gully
      at a grassy corner 30 feet below the start of The Crack.

(1)   35 feet. Step up the grass terrace sloping to the right and
      traverse 10 feet farther right to cross a steep wall.
      Climb slightly leftwards up the wall via a pointed flake
      to a good grass ledge farther left, with belay above.

(2)   20 feet. Follow a series of steps running up to the right
      to a small grass nook with good jammed belay.

(3)   25 feet. Climb straight up for 5 feet, traverse horizontally
      left for a few feet, then up again to a small juniper
      ledge. At this level traverse horizontally right to the

ridge which in a few feet leads to a poorish stance with, however, good belays.

(4) 45 feet. This pitch is the hardest, though the difficulty is of short duration. A short diagonal ascent to the left is made to the foot of a thin crack slanting left. This is climbed, holds being small at first but soon improving and the top is reached without further difficulty. Belay some distance back up the grass terrace. (Instead of the thin crack, the wall a few feet farther left may be climbed on improving holds.) It is possible to escape to the right from the foot of the final pitch, crossing North-west Arête *en route*.

SAMARITAN CORNER.—130 feet. Very severe. A companion route to Asterisk, and of similar standard, following the line of the obvious corner on its left. Starts just to the left of Asterisk in the right-angled corner.

(1) 30 feet. The corner is climbed to a grass shelf. Step right and up to a ledge and belay at the top of Pitch 1, Asterisk.

(2) 20 feet. The groove on the left is entered by an awkward move and followed to a stance and belay.

(3) 40 feet. Continue up the corner to a grass-topped bulge. This is turned on the vertical right wall. A belay is reached in the grassy groove above.

(4) 40 feet. The wall on the right is climbed to the top. The belay is some distance away at the back of the grass ledge.

NORTH-WEST FACE (Upper Section)

THE CRACK.—240 feet. Very severe. A first-rate climb, one of the classic routes of the Lake District. A reasonable

standard is maintained throughout. Starts a few fee[
above Samaritan Corner in the North-west Gully a[
the foot of a grassy groove which soon merges int[
the Crack proper.

(1)　30 feet.　An easy scramble up the groove leads to a gras[
　　　　ledge.　Thread-belay on the left.

(2)　25 feet.　The narrow crack above, steepening as it rises[
　　　　offers good hand and toe holds.　An awkward stanc[
　　　　is reached with a good flake-belay on the left.

(3)　30 feet.　Step on to the belay and traverse 10 feet to th[
　　　　left on two small flakes when good handholds facilitat[
　　　　a delicate move round the corner into a groove.　Th[
　　　　groove is climbed, veering left at the top, to a gras[
　　　　ledge and pedestal belay.　(A very strenuous alternativ[
　　　　to the traverse is to continue up the crack for 15 fee[
　　　　from the belay before moving left to the pedestal.)

(4)　25 feet.　From the top of the pedestal a narrow crack lead[
　　　　up to the left to a delicate mantelshelf.　(Useful side[
　　　　holds in the thin crack above.)　An upward travers[
　　　　to the left is followed to a comfortable corner anc[
　　　　large belay.

(5)　20 feet.　The steep ridge on the right is climbed on goo[
　　　　holds after a preliminary pull-up.　Spike-belay.

(6)　25 feet.　Traverse easily back right into the crack anc[
　　　　ascend to the Sentry Box.　Flake-belay rather low[
　　　　on the left.

(7)　15 feet.　A strenuous pull-up leads to a good ledge on the[
　　　　right (The Bower).　Awkward thread belay.

(8)　40 feet.　Straight up the crack to the Overhang (chock-
　　　　stone for running belay).　Facing right, a foothold high[
　　　　on the right wall can eventually be employed to assist[

the pull-over. A few feet higher a small stance and thread-belay are reached.

9) 30 feet. Continue up the chimney to the top. It is possible to escape to the right at 15 feet.

HIATUS.—325 feet. Very Severe. A tedious introduction relieved by a magnificent finish. The climb runs up the grassy slabs to the left of The Crack as far as the final prominent overhangs. These are turned on the left by an exposed traverse. Starts 6 feet to the left of the foot of The Crack.

1) 25 feet. A steep wall is climbed to a terrace and belay.

2) 15 feet. An easy grassy traverse upwards to the left leads to a corner with belay on the right.

3) 35 feet. An awkward scoop round the corner on the right is followed by the ridge on its left to the pedestal belay on The Crack.

4) 30 feet. Step across to a mantelshelf and slab on the left, leading to another grass shelf and belays.

5) 55 feet. The grassy gully ahead is followed for 30 feet until a terrace leads off to the left to a small tree and line belays.

6) 50 feet. Another terrace leads back right into the gully which is forsaken after a few feet for a traverse left across a mossy wall to ledges and belays. There is is also an excellent thread-belay 10 feet higher.

7) 70 feet. Work up the mossy gully into the right-hand corner, then step across a large, loose block and follow a rising traverse left over a delicate slab below the overhangs. Good holds are reached beneath a steep corner. This is climbed for 10 feet, when two steps to the left, first up, then down, bring good holds

into use for the continuance of the traverse under a
pointed, overhanging rib to a second rib. This is
climbed direct for 10 feet to a fine niche with splendid
belay above on the right.

(8) 45 feet. The slab on the left and a short awkward scoop
are followed by scrambling to the top.

Bridge's Variation.

(7a) 70 feet. From the steep corner on the ordinary route
climb straight up and over the rib into the same niche.

(8a) 40 feet. The steep, black-looking chimney above leads
to the summit. The jammed block appears to be
sound but should be treated with respect. This
variation is appreciably harder than the ordinary
finish but of similar character.

VARIATION FINISH—GROOVES TRAVERSE.—Very severe.
Much harder than the ordinary finish, the overhangs
being turned on the right instead of on the left. Starts
from the foot of the penultimate pitch of Hiatus.

(1) 60 feet. Pitch 7 of the ordinary route is followed to the
level of the large loose block. A rather strenuous 20-
foot traverse is then made across the steep wall on the
right into a groove which leads without difficulty to a
small stance beneath a mossy scoop. Thread-belay
(for line only) above on the left. A running belay can
be arranged at the commencement of the traverse
round a somewhat friable flake.

(2) 50 feet. The mossy scoop is climbed for 5 feet when a
very delicate traverse is made to the right for 15 feet
beneath a small overhang. A groove slanting right is
reached and climbed on good holds to the top. Fine
belays.

GROOVES SUPERDIRECT.—Very severe. One of the hardest
pitches in the district, but well protected. Avoids
the final traverse on Grooves Traverse by the ascent
of the mossy scoop.

(1) 45 feet. From the belay at the foot of the final pitch of
Grooves Traverse the scoop is climbed for 5 feet when
a step left is made to a small foothold on the mossy
slab. A tiny flake is then reached at full stretch (it
affords a useful running belay for nylon line only)
with the aid of which a delicate step into the shallow
groove on the left can be made. Move left again and
ascend on improving holds back to the right into the
main groove which is climbed to the top without
further difficulty.

GODIVA GROOVE.—190 feet. Very severe. A natural route,
somewhat exposed in its upper section. The most
obvious weakness in the North-west Face to the left
of Hiatus is a V-groove which starts high up the North-
west Gully and finishes just to the left of the final
scoop of Hiatus ; its easy middle section is used by
Juniper Buttress. The climb takes a more or less
direct line up this groove. The start is reached by
scrambling out of the North-west Gully to a grass
ledge below the left-bounding rib of the groove.

(1) 30 feet. A rising traverse to the right leads into the
groove which is climbed to a stance and flake-belay.

(2) 50 feet. Ascend the groove for 15 feet when a long, awkward stride can be made across the left wall to a ledge
on the corner. Avoiding the loose block which rests
here, follow the rib, then the groove again, to a stance
and belay just above the junction with Juniper Buttress.

(3) 30 feet. Continue up Juniper Buttress (Pitch 3) to a
     belay in the groove.

(4) 80 feet. After a few feet in the groove work up on to the
     left wall and climb direct to the overhang. This is
     overcome by moving left into another mossy groove
     when a steep but broken wall leads to the top.   (An
     alternative finish is to climb the clean rib on the right
     of the belay to a large spike on a ledge when a move
     to the right leads to the belay below the last pitch
     of Hiatus. Finish up this.)

JUNIPER BUTTRESS.—190 feet. Severe in boots. A pleasant
     climb, deserving greater popularity, on the right
     bounding wall of Junipall Gully. The start is reached
     by scrambling out to the right a little above the bottom
     of the Gully to a terrace just below, and to the right
     of, a small ash-tree.

(1) 45 feet. The rib immediately to the right of the ash-tree
     is followed, mostly on its left edge, to a large flake-
     belay in a grassy gully on the left.

(2) 50 feet. Traverse horizontally right for 30 feet, passing
     an unsafe block, to a corner under a nose. Climb
     over the nose into a V-groove which is ascended
     (avoiding a doubtful block) until good holds on the
     rib on the right lead to a small stance. Excellent belay
     high up on the right.

(3) 25 feet. Continue up the rib until a short traverse left,
     crossing a grassy gully, leads to a ledge and belays.

(4) 30 feet. Traverse left along juniper ledges and across
     a slab. Then ascend a little, step across an awkward
     corner and round a rib to a comfortable recess.

     One can walk off left at this point into Junipall Gully.

5) 40 feet. Ascend the steep rib on the right on good holds. Small handholds on the flat top facilitate the landing, whence scrambling leads to the top.

UNIPALL GULLY.—The gully separating the North-west Face from Pallid Buttress. It turns at right angles out of North-west Gully and leads to the top of Gimmer, finishing a few yards short of the top of South-east Gully. Usually wet, and containing much loose scree and one or two moderate pitches, it is a convenient means of descent to the north-west side of the Crag.

PALLID BUTTRESS

NOCTURNE.—190 feet. Very severe. A pleasantly exposed route up the left wall of the gully. The crack used on the second pitch is just to the left of an obvious streak of black moss. Starts in the gully a few feet above the lowest point of the buttress and below a prominent line of overhangs.

1) 60 feet. Ascend left towards a rib, to the point where a mossy crack provides the only breach in the overhang. Fairly good holds are available for the pull-over. Work rightwards to a good ledge with small belay above (junction with top of Pitch 1, Pallid Slabs).

The same ledge may be reached more easily by starting higher up the gully, a few yards below its first short chimney pitch, and following a zigzag crack to the left. This was the original start.

Yet another alternative is to avoid the ledge entirely by climbing a groove immediately to the right of the original start until a step left leads to a junction with the second pitch at the right-hand end of the hand-traverse.

(2)   90 feet.   Ascend directly on good holds until progress is stopped by the overhang.   This is turned by a short hand-traverse to the right followed by a vertical ascent up a shallow crack (good spike for running belay). The holds become small and relief is found by traversing back left above the overhang on to better, but mossy, holds.   A grassy recess is reached with flake-belay.

(3)   40 feet.   Ascend diagonally left to a small ledge on the arête, then up a mossy corner on the right to a heather ledge.   A thin crack is followed by a rightward movement when easier climbing and scrambling lead to the top.

PALLID SLABS.—185 feet.   Severe.   A route providing delicate climbing of considerable quality.   Starts a short distance to the left of Nocturne, from the top of a large juniper and bilberry-covered boulder.

(1)   65 feet.   Step onto the slabs from the boulder and traverse upwards to the right under a series of small overhangs to a good ledge with small line belay above (junction with Nocturne).

(2)   50 feet.   The wall a few feet left of the belay is climbed direct to a ' junipiferous and heathery ' ledge on the left.   The last few feet are particularly delicate.   A good block-belay hides low down in the heather on the left of this ledge (The Haven).

(3)   50 feet.   Step round into a groove from the left edge of the ledge, and proceed via the right wall of a miniature

cave up heather ledges to a corner and belay below a steep crack.

20 feet. Follow the crack to the finishing ledge.

LEFACE.—155 feet. Severe. A climb of increasing interest with a fine finish. Starts midway between Pallid Slabs and the left-hand corner of the main buttress below a shallow chimney.

25 feet. Indefinite mossy rocks lead to a belay at the foot of a heather-topped, shallow chimney.

25 feet. The heather ledge is gained by a direct ascent to the left of the belay and an awkward step to the right. Spike-belay above on the left.

25 feet. Stepping over the spike, climb the steep, mossy wall to a stance on a rock ledge to the right. Belay on the left.

80 feet. From the right-hand end of the ledge ascend direct to the overhang, passing in 25 feet a large heather recess. The overhang is circumvented by an exhilarating traverse to the right leading up to a flat ledge where a block has come away, and an easy traverse back to the left. The 15-foot wall above is climbed on sloping holds to an abrupt finish.

ALL END.—125 feet. Severe. The easiest of the routes on this buttress. Starts at the foot of a rib forming the left-hand end of the main Pallid Buttress. A gully runs up to the left.

55 feet. The rib is climbed until its steepening necessitates a stride onto a heather ledge on the right. Traverse 20 feet to the foot of a vertical V-groove

which is climbed on good holds to a comfortab
niche. Belay on the right.

(2) 40 feet. A diagonal ascent to the left leads to an awkwa
landing onto a sloping ledge. A large ledge 15 fe
higher is attained by climbing the steep wall abov
Belay on left.

(3) 30 feet. Easy slabs above or a more difficult groove
the right.

ASHEN TRAVERSE.—205 feet. Very severe. Girdles Pall
Buttress from right to left, finishing up a smooth sl.
on the subsidiary crag beyond Wall End. The fir
pitch is the principal difficulty but the final slab,
crack, is an entertaining problem. Starts from
grass ledge in Junipall Gully at the top of its fir
chimney pitch.

(1) 70 feet. The first objective is a large flake immediate
to the right of a conspicuous streak of black mos
It is gained by a 15-foot traverse across the wall
satisfying holds. From the flake, where a runnir
belay can be arranged, a very awkward step is take
across the moss to the shallow crack on the secon
pitch of Nocturne. The crack is followed for a fe
feet until it is possible to traverse left round a corne
and across a slab to the heathery ledge at the top o
the second pitch of Pallid Slabs.

(2) 30 feet. From the left-hand end of the ledge continu
the traverse across a chimney. A rounded rock ledg
then leads to a nook, complete with belay.

(3) 40 feet. Step round the corner and attain a ledge whic
slopes downwards to the left. This is followed pas

a groove until a long stride leads round into a large,
grassy recess below an imposing crack.

•) 65 feet. Crimson Crack. The crack may be followed
throughout, using poor footholds on the left wall,
or, more pleasantly, after 15 feet in the crack work
diagonally left across the wall for a few feet, then
straight up to the top. A grassy corner leads to a good
belay.

'HE GIRDLE TRAVERSE.—675 feet. Very severe. A magnificent
expedition, traversing the whole of the main Buttress
from South-east Gully to Junipall Gully. The climbing is almost continuously exacting and exposed,
especially across the North-west Face. Though
complete in itself and quite arduous enough, the
Traverse may very suitably be extended to include
Pallid Buttress by means of Ashen Traverse. Starts
in South-east Gully at the foot of Bachelor Crack.

1) 20 feet. The first pitch of Bachelor Crack.

2) 50 feet. Surmount the bulging wall above and follow
a horizontal traverse to the left, first delicately across
slabs and an awkward groove, then easily to the belay
above the twin chimneys (top of Pitch 6, Gimmer
Chimney).

3) 40 feet. Continue round the corner and over easy rocks
to a belay overlooking the Gangway.

4) 40 feet. Step down a few feet and cross the impending
wall to the Gangway by a descending hand-traverse
(part of Pitch 5, Crow's Nest Direct, reversed).
Continue up the Gangway to the belay at the foot
of Green Chimney.

(5) 40 feet. Take the easiest line leftwards to the foot of Lichen Chimney. Belay.

(6) 45 feet. Musgrave's Traverse is followed across the steep wall to the belay below the Forked Lightning Crack on ' D.'

(7) 50 feet. Hyphen, Pitch 2, is reversed.

(8) 35 feet. Pitch 2, Kipling Groove.

(9) 40 feet. From the recess descend 15 feet when good holds permit a traverse to be made into a groove on the left. The groove is climbed with difficulty until a pull-out to the left and a short ascent lead to the Bower on The Crack. Block-belay, or thread-belay in the crack ; most awkward to fix.

(10) 40 feet. The Crack is climbed past the Overhang to the small stance and thread belay (Pitch 8).

(11) 45 feet. A few feet higher on the left a line of holds lead horizontally across the wall for 10 feet to a steep corner bounded on the left by an overhung groove. The corner is climbed, using good but distantly spaced holds on the right wall, until it is possible to work diagonally left to a stance and belay in a broken groove (This is the final groove of Grooves Traverse.)

(12) 30 feet. After a step down a very delicate traverse leads just below a small, but conspicuous, overhang into a mossy scoop which is descended to a stance and thread belay for line only. (Part of Pitch 2, Grooves Traverse, reversed.)

(13) 45 feet. Pitch 1, Grooves Traverse is reversed to the large, detached block on Hiatus, which is used for belay. It can be supplemented by the flake at the end of the traverse.

(14) 50 feet. Continue up Hiatus (The Traverse) to the good niche and belay.

(15) 35 feet. Move round the corner to the left, passing a large spike, and pull across an open chimney onto good holds. After one step down an easy traverse leads to the belay at the top of Pitch 3, Juniper Buttress.

(16) 30 feet. Pitch 4, Juniper Buttress is followed to the edge of Junipall Gully. (The start of Ashen Traverse is immediately across the Gully.)

(17) 40 feet. The last pitch of Juniper Buttress leads pleasantly to the top of the Crag.

WHITE GHYLL CRAG

The Approaches

Situated in Great Langdale, White Ghyll lies parallel to Mill Ghyll, a bare half-mile to the east. It rises steeply from a point a few hundred yards short of the New Hotel, ill-defined at first but boldly modelled near the sky-line, where the Crag, towering grandly above its narrow, stony bed, presents a most striking picture as seen from the valley.

The climbs may be reached from the main road in less than half-an-hour. From the New Hotel cross the stream behind the hotel and follow a rising track across the fields until the Ghyll is reached. Ascending directly up the Ghyll from here, a steep outcrop on the left (Swine Knott) is passed and, soon afterwards, a sycamore gained. This is the usual base for the Lower Crag which now rises immediately on the right.

If approaching from the lower reaches of the dale, it is best to turn off the road directly below Scout Crag and follow the track to its summit, when an indefinite trod leads round to the left and into the Ghyll just below the sycamore.

Topographical

White Ghyll Crag forms the right bank of the Ghyll for a considerable distance from its summit and, for convenience of description, can be separated into an upper and a lower section, the dividing mark being some 40 yards above the prominent sycamore, where a grassy rake (the left-hand one of a pair) slants up to the right, drops a little onto a broad, grass shelf (The Great Shelf), then rises smoothly to the top ; this is Easy Rake, a convenient means of descent.

The Upper Crag is split by a narrow, but imposing fissure, White Ghyll Chimney. On the left of the Chimney is a fine sweep of slabs, on the right a most aggressive-looking wall, protected at half-height by a series of formidable overhangs which hardly relent until the right-hand terminus of the wall at Easy Rake. The routes on this wall give some of the finest climbing in the district.

The Lower Crag begins, on the left, as a steep, but short, wall, topped by a secondary tier of rock from which it is separated by the Great Shelf. It then becomes broken into a number of sharply-defined grooves—almost all of which give short climbs of considerable quality—finally merging into the hellside at the entrance to the Ghyll. The Lower Crag is naturally endowed with a fairly liberal mantle of vegetation, but a recent fire has removed the greater part of it. The resulting denudation has not materially affected the various climbs, except in requiring extra care at one or two points where unstable soil has replaced the more reliable turf and in making some of the names temporarily inappropriate. However, pending a return to its normal verdancy, terms such as ' a grassy scramble ' may indicate a decidedly earthy crawl.

The standard of the climbs, both in difficulty and quality, is generally high ; the rock is adequately cohesive, the situations often unique. The climbs are described from right to left, that is as seen when ascending the Ghyll.

LOWER CRAG

The first feature of note is a prominent ridge, Junction Arête. On its right The Sidings offer a few short pitches of moderate difficulty preceded by an unpleasantly earthy scramble up the side of the Ghyll.

JUNCTION ARÊTE.—150 feet. Severe (Difficult if the firs
 pitch is avoided). Two oaks in a groove on the righ
 help to identify a route of some interest. Starts a
 the foot of the ridge.

(1) 60 feet. After a 25-foot glacis an overhang gives food fo
 thought. Bridging brings a high handhold into reach
 when an awkward move over to the right leads t
 easier ground. Continue up to a stance and bela
 opposite the first oak.

(2) 25 feet. The ridge ahead. Stance and belay level wit
 the second oak.

(3) 25 feet. Less easily up to a capacious ledge (Th
 Platform).

(4) 40 feet. Straight on without incident to the top of th
 Crag.

 Junction Arête is bounded on the left by a broad, cracke
 wall. Beyond this commences a series of open groove
 The next two climbs start at the same point, a larg
 block at the foot of the second groove ; it is reache
 by scrambling up broken rocks a few yards to the lef
 of Junction Arête. The first climb rejects the stee
 V-groove immediately above the block in favour o
 the similar, but less challenging, fault away to th
 right. Heather Groove remedies that defect. Bot
 routes provide interesting climbing.

RUSSET GROOVE.—90 feet. Severe.

(1) 40 feet. From the foot of the block an easy slab slant
 up to the right. A good stance and belay are reache
 in the groove.

(2) 50 feet. Small holds in the groove lead in 20 feet to

ledge out on the right wall. The short, steep wall above on the left is then climbed to the top.

HEATHER GROOVE.—90 feet. Severe.
(1) 40 feet. The overhanging corner above the block is climbed to a small ledge below a slab. The slab is then ascended to a stance and belay on its left-hand edge.
(2) 50 feet. Return to the right-hand side of the slab and climb direct to the top.

INFERNO.—210 feet. Very severe. Takes the groove next to Heather Groove, conspicuous with its overhang at 30 feet. Rather broken rocks below the groove provide two introductory pitches. The climbing is interesting throughout. Starts directly beneath the groove, just below a tiny pitch in the bed of the Ghyll.
(1) 40 feet. Straight up to an overhang which is overcome by means of a short crack. Ledge and belay.
(2) 50 feet. The rib ahead leads to a terrace below the groove.
(3) 80 feet. The groove is climbed to the overhang mainly by bridging. It is now possible to ' chimney ' up past the overhang, when difficulties ease and a grass ledge on the right is soon gained. Belay. One can leave the climb at this point.
(4) 40 feet. Step back left into the groove and ascend to the top, avoiding a loose block.

DO NOT.—115 feet. Very severe. Considerably harder than anything else in the Ghyll. Lies up the left wall of the unclimbed groove between Inferno and Slip Knot and uses the tree-belay on the latter. Starts at a belay in the groove reached by scrambling up from the bed of the Ghyll.

(1) 45 feet. The groove is climbed for about 20 feet, when it is possible to move onto the bulging left wall and so up to a roomy ledge and holly-tree-belay (Junction with Slip Knot). The holds on the wall gradually deteriorate and a crack, slanting up to the left, is used for both an underhand grip and an awkward knee-jam. The final moves onto the ledge are very strenuous.

(2) 70 feet. The square-cut groove above on the right is climbed on small, but sufficient, holds to an overhang. Traverse left across the wall onto the nose when an awkward balance upwards brings good holds into reach. The top and a belay are then reached without difficulty. This pitch is very exposed, but a running belay can be arranged on the first foothold of the traverse across the wall.

SLIP KNOT.—125 feet. Very severe. Just to the left of Do Not and immediately above the sycamore in the Ghyll is a conspicuous right-angled corner, topped by a large, triangular overhang. The climb runs up the right wall of the corner and turns the overhang on the left. Starts at the foot of the corner.

(1) 60 feet. After a few feet in the corner excellent holds lead up the right wall to a good ledge and holly-tree-belay (junction with Do Not). A thin crack, containing a withered tree, is used for the ascent of the final section of the wall.

(2) 65 feet. Work leftwards into the corner over shattered rocks and make an awkward stride out to the far rib. An overhang is climbed to a grassy recess on the left.

Step out right from here and climb the face above the overhang to the top. Small belay immediately above and a better one 20 feet up to the right. Note.—A pleasant alternative to the beginning of the pitch is to descend 10 feet from the belay and traverse across to the rib at that level. This was the original route.

GARDEN PATH.—150 feet. Very difficult. Lies up the broken-looking buttress, conspicuous because of the triangular niche in the middle of its steepest section, a short way up the Ghyll from the sycamore. The grassy finish requires some care. Starts at a cairn about 15 feet above the tree.

(1) 45 feet. The wall is climbed on good holds past a small ash-tree to a large grass ledge. Belay on wall above.

(2) 15 feet. The obvious rock niche above on the left is gained by rather awkward climbing. Good thread belay in top left corner.

(3) 45 feet. Move round the corner on the left to a small ledge, then back right onto the face above the niche. Continue straight up to a large heather shelf. Spike-belay higher on left.

(4) 45 feet. Unpleasant heathery scrambling leads to a large ledge and pinnacle-belay. Either escape to the right, finish up the last pitch of Why Not (q.v.), or traverse left into Easy Rake.

WHY NOT.—150 feet. Very difficult. Lies up the broad scoop just beyond Garden Path and 20 feet to the right of Hollin Groove. Perhaps the best of the easier climbs in the Ghyll. Starts at the foot of the scoop.

(1) 30 feet. Easily up to a stance. Belay on left.

(2) 40 feet. Climb over the belay and up to stance and belay level with the holly-tree on Hollin Groove.

(3) 25 feet. Step right and ascend to an opening in the overhang above. This is climbed with some difficulty and leads to a large ledge and belay.

(4) 25 feet. Steep grass to a huge, detached pinnacle. Belay.

(5) 30 feet. The groove on the left of the pinnacle leads to the top. Alternatively one can step off the top of the pinnacle and climb the severe slab ahead to the same point.

HOLLIN GROOVE.—265 feet. Severe. Lies up the conspicuous V-groove some 50 feet up the Ghyll from the sycamore. A natural route as far as the Great Shelf which unfortunately breaks the continuity, although the ridge above is not without interest. Starts at the foot of a short, clean groove,

(1) 20 feet. Climb the groove, with difficulty at first, to a turf stance and embedded flake-belay.

(2) 25 feet. Step onto the rib on the left, then straight up to a stance. Spike-belay on right.

(3) 30 feet. The vertical groove above the stance is followed by a move left into the corner. Holly-tree-belay. Alternatively the holly-tree can be attained by climbing the easier groove immediately beneath it.

(4) 80 feet. The right-angled groove above leads pleasantly up to the Great Shelf. Walk 40 feet to a belay on the rib ahead.

(5) 35 feet. The steep rib is climbed to a stance and spike-belay.

(6) 75 feet. Continue up the rib to the top.

GRANNY KNOT.—130 feet. Severe. (Very difficult by alternative exit.) A good face climb, quite exposed in its
upper section. The overhang is turned on the right
unless the easier finish is taken. Starts 30 feet to the
left of Hollin Groove, below and to the right of a
large, rectangular overhang.

1) 70 feet. A steep rib is climbed to a stance and belay
level with a small mountain-ash. There is a way off
on the left.

2) 60 feet. Traverse 15 feet to the right on large holds, then
ascend direct over an awkward bulge and up an airy
ridge to finish on the Great Shelf.

Variation finish : The groove above the belay is climbed
to the overhang when a short traverse left leads to
easy ground just below the Great Shelf.

Between Granny Knot and the Upper Crag is the grassy
thoroughfare of Easy Rake (see Topography).

UPPER CRAG

WHITE GHYLL WALL.—220 feet. Very severe. The easiest of
the routes on the central mass, the overhangs being
turned on the right. Some fine situations. Starts at
the foot of a prominent rib, just to the right of a small
cave below a withered ash-tree.

(1) 30 feet. Up the rib to a stance below a split rock. Thread-
belay in crack.

(2) 25 feet. The rib again to a ledge and belay beneath the
overhang.

(3) 25 feet. Traverse easily to the right to a stance and belay
at the foot of an undercut scoop.

(4) 25 feet. The scoop is climbed to a small stance but good
belay, an overhang halfway proving awkward.

(5) 25 feet. Step left onto the steep, mossy wall and ascend direct for 20 feet, when it is possible to move left into a small recess. Belay.

(6) 40 feet. Climb delicately leftwards up the steep slab to a ledge and small belay. (It is possible to avoid this and succeeding pitches by climbing the broken groove which runs up to the top of the Crag. As an alternative it gives inferior climbing.)

(7) 20 feet. Easier rocks lead diagonally left to the grass ledge below the final pitch of the Gordian Knot.

(8) 30 feet. The wall above is climbed on good holds to the top.

PERHAPS NOT.—205 feet. Very severe. Turns the first series of overhangs by using the same start as White Ghyll Wall ; a very exposed traverse to the left enables the final barrier to be overcome by the most trying pitch in the Ghyll, always excepting Do Not. Starts at the foot of the rib below the withered ash.

(1) 30 feet. ⎫
(2) 25 feet. ⎬ As for White Ghyll Wall.

(3) 50 feet. Climb up to the overhang, then traverse left underneath it to the foot of an overhung chimney. Belay. This is exposed work throughout on rock that is not above suspicion.

(4) 30 feet. The chimney is climbed with great difficulty (faith in what may be above is required when the holds disappear) until one can step out right below the overhang and ascend to a stance and belay.

(5) 40 feet. Continue straight up the wall to the grass ledge below the final pitches of the Gordian Knot and White Ghyll Wall.

(6) 30 feet. The wall above.

THE GORDIAN KNOT.—190 feet. Very severe. A natural climb
of great character. All difficulties can be adequately
protected, but the second pitch is not to be won easily
at first acquaintance.   Starts about 20 yards to the
right of the Chimney, at the foot of a narrow slab
which runs in a single sweep up to the main overhang.

(1) 65 feet. Straight up the slab, tending rightwards until
its steepening necessitates a rising traverse to the left
edge. Work up and right from here to a cave below
the overhang. Horizontal belay at the back and a
sloping spike farther right ; used in opposition they
form a safe anchorage.

(2) 30 feet. An easy traverse leads round to the right for 15
feet to a good ledge below a mossy corner. (It is
possible to belay here.) The corner is climbed, passing
a good spike for a running belay, until it is possible to
gain with hands or feet a tiny ledge on the right wall.
Whatever method is employed these few feet are the
hardest on the climb. From a standing position on the
ledge pull up on good holds and move back left into
a recess complete with belay.

(3) 15 feet. The rather strenuous corner ahead is climbed
to a ledge and belay.

(4) 40 feet. Easier climbing with an exit onto a broad grass
ledge. Belay 20 feet along the ledge.

(5) 40 feet. The wall above.

HASTE NOT.—185 feet. Very severe. An exposed climb of a
high, and well-maintained, standard of difficulty up
the impending wall to the left of the Gordian Knot.

E

Starts about 20 feet to the left of the latter, at the foot of a short, overhung slab.

(1) 20 feet. Easily up the slab to a stance and belay beneath an inverted V-overhang.

(2) 50 feet. Break out onto the left wall and, with difficulty, step round into a groove on its bounding slab. Continue straight up this over an awkward bulge to a ledge level with the top of the first pitch of the Chimney. Belay.

(3) 15 feet. An easy traverse to the right leads to a belay above a steep slab. (Part of Pitch 15, White Ghyll Traverse, reversed.)

(4) 30 feet. A sensational pitch. Ascend the wall directly above the belay until it is possible to make a delicate step onto a gangway running to the right under the huge overhang. Traverse the gangway and make a difficult move into a groove below an impending corner. Swing over the corner to a belay opposite the top of Pitch 3 on the Gordian Knot. (One may move across and use the better stance on this climb if preferred.)

(5) 70 feet. Starting just to the right of the belay, the wall above is climbed with some difficulty. Continue up between two overhanging blocks to the top of the Crag.

WHITE GHYLL CHIMNEY.—185 feet. Severe. A classic route of considerable merit up the impressive cleft between the central overhangs and the slabs. Starts at the foot of the obvious, grassy groove just to the right of the Slabs.

(1) 45 feet. Up the steepening groove without difficulty to

an exit on the right. A terrace is reached with a good
block-belay.

?) 20 feet. Walk up the grass to a thread-belay in the
Sentry Box, above which the chimney narrows to a
crack.

?) 80 feet. Ascend the cave for 10 feet and make a very
awkward movement to a sloping hold on the left.
Balance over to reach small handholds and continue
more easily up a steep groove, tending leftwards, to
a grass ledge. 20 feet farther up this is a good belay.

?a) A more difficult, but often drier, alternative is to
avoid the chimney entirely by climbing the wall on its
left. From the belay in the Sentry Box step down a
few feet and traverse left across the wall for 15 feet.
A direct ascent on smaller holds then leads to the same
diagonal groove. Continue up this to the belay.

?) 40 feet. Return 10 feet from the belay and ascend the
wall above for 15 feet. A delicate traverse leads back
into the chimney, which is followed to the top.

THE SLABS, ROUTE I.—225 feet. Severe in boots. Both the
Slab routes offer pleasant climbing on steep, sound
rock, well supplied with holds. Route I is a little the
harder. Starts at the lowest part of the buttress.

.) 40 feet. Bubbly rocks lead to a ledge with belay at its
left end. Stance below.

?) 20 feet. Traverse upwards across the wall on the left to a
small ledge with flake-belay above.

?) 30 feet. The steep groove above is climbed until one can
move out to the right to a splendid spike-belay.

?) 55 feet. Attack the wall above, 10 feet to the left of the
belay. After an awkward start better holds lead via

the middle one of three steep grooves to a ledge runnin
right. Thence by a groove on the right to the terrac
which runs out from above the third pitch of Whi
Ghyll Chimney.

(5) 80 feet. A few feet to the right of the belay is a steep ril
Start slightly to the right of this, then follow the ri
to the top of the Crag. This pitch may be avoided b
unpleasant heathery scrambling on the left.

THE SLABS, ROUTE 2.—145 feet. Severe in boots. Starts a
the left end of the buttress, below its bounding ridg

(1) 35 feet. A steep crack, just to the right, leads to the stanc
and belay above the second pitch of Route 1.

(2) 30 feet. Traverse horizontally left across the wall unt
a good, high spike facilitates a pull-up onto the sla
above. Continue diagonally right to the spike-bela
above pitch 3, Route 1.

(3) 45 feet. After retracing one's steps for 20 feet, the wa
above is climbed by a crack running diagonally lef
when the ridge farther left leads to a stance and bela

(4) 35 feet. Follow the ridge on the right of the grassy scoo
above.
80 feet of scrambling finishes the climb.

ALTERNATIVE START.—65 feet. Rather harder than th
original route. Starts at the foot of an open chimne
on the immediate left of the Slabs proper.

(1) 25 feet. Bridge up the chimney until it is possible t
step out onto the slab on the left. Turf ledges ar
reached with a flake-belay suitable for line only.

(2) 40 feet. Traverse right along small grass ledges and cros
a delicate slab to a junction with the second pitc

of the ordinary route. Continue up this to the spike-belay. It is probably better to combine these two pitches.

WHITE GHYLL TRAVERSE.—About 600 feet of climbing. Very severe. A most attractive expedition offering a fair taste of some of the best climbing on the Crag. The easiest practicable line is followed from Hollin Groove to the far edge of the Slabs. Starts at the foot of Hollin Groove.

(1-4) The first four pitches of Hollin Groove (q.v.) lead to the Great Shelf.

(5) 50 feet. Scramble easily up to the left to a block-belay above the first steep section of Easy Rake.

(6) 70 feet. Take the easiest line leftwards to the block-belay at the foot of Pitch 4, White Ghyll Wall.

(7-10) The next four pitches of White Ghyll Wall lead up the undercut scoop and diagonally left to the grass ledge below the final pitch.

(11-13) Pitches 4, 3 and 2 of the Gordian Knot reversed. The descent of the mossy corner is probably the hardest part of the Traverse ; it is, however, easier than its ascent.

(14) 45 feet. Traverse left from the cave across the top of an undercut groove and so to a slab which is climbed to its top left-hand corner. Belay.

(15) 25 feet. The block-belay at the top of the first pitch of the Chimney is reached by an easy traverse.

(16) 90 feet. Continue the traverse with difficulty, first ascending to a shattered ledge, where a running belay can be arranged, then descending delicately to the

arête whence good holds lead diagonally left to the
spike-belay above Pitch 3, Route 1.

(17) 45 feet. Work obliquely left to the belay at the top of
Pitch 3, Route 2.

(18) 35 feet. Pitch 4, Route 2. Scrambling for 80 feet leads
to the top of the Crag.

PORKERS' PARADE.—145 feet. Severe. Owing to some doubt
as to the exact line taken by this route, the following
is adapted from a description by R. J. Birkett. Lies
on Swine Knott, the steep little outcrop on the left
of the entrance to the Ghyll. Starts at the lowest
point of the crag on the White Ghyll side.

(1) 25 feet. Straight up the arête to a stance and belay on a
ledge to the right of a yew-tree.

(2) 120 feet. Ascend direct from the middle of the ledge for
12 feet, then traverse left round an overhanging corner
to an arête which is followed to the top of the crag.

PAVEY ARK

THE APPROACHES

GREAT LANGDALE.—From the New Hotel, Pavey Ark is approached by ascending Mill Ghyll. There is a track on each side of the ghyll but the left one is more commonly used. On reaching Stickle Tarn the crag appears in full view. From here the drier and shorter route is on the left of the tarn and afterwards indefinite tracks lead up the scree to the foot of the crag.

From the Old Hotel one can traverse the fellside either high or low. If one ascends Middlefell Buttress, then the undulating plateau below Harrison Stickle is followed to the right, Dungeon Ghyll is crossed (here not very deeply incut), and the grassy shoulder ahead leads one out above Stickle Tarn. To traverse low below the various outcrops, a track runs along behind the wall and leads, still quite low, into that following the left side of Mill Ghyll whence the route is identical with the one from the New Hotel.

From White Ghyll Crags ascend the Ghyll and take a direct line to the foot of the Tarn where the Mill Ghyll route is joined.

BORROWDALE.—The route to Gimmer Crag is followed, and from the top continued in the same direction over the col to the north of Harrison Stickle, so arriving above the Tarn.

TOPOGRAPHICAL

The crag in general faces south and enjoys rather more, and more varied, vegetation than most of the Lakeland crags. It is the largest cliff in Langdale, a factor which, together with its fine situation above Stickle Tarn, compensates somewhat for the occasional shortcomings of the rock itself. It is split by gullies into several distinct buttresses. Those to the left of Great Gully, the second deeply-cut gully from the left, are neither steep nor sound, but broken and unsuitable for good climbing. Stony Buttress comes next between Great Gully and a shallow, dirt-filled groove which marks the line of ascent to the Crescent (the signs of a recent rock-fall are conspicuous hereabouts). Next comes a sweep of smooth slabs, bordered above and down to the right by a series of grassy ledges which form a rake (Jack's Rake) leading from high up on the western end of the crags down to the scree at the eastern extremity. The buttress above Jack's Rake, up which lie Bracken Route and Cook's Tour, is split on the left by Gwynne's Chimney and bounded on the right by the well-defined Rake End Chimney. Beyond the latter is the East Buttress which presents a bold front to the south and a series of intimidating (and unclimbed) grooves to the east.

Many climbs lead only to Jack's Rake, which serves as an easy means of descent. From the summit a descent can be made round either extremity, or, more easily, via the easier upper section of Great Gully to Jack's Rake and then down the latter. Rake End Chimney provides a pleasant means of descent after climbing on the eastern end of the crag, though care is needed to avoid dislodging scree on to ascending parties.

THE CLIMBS

LITTLE GULLY.—350 feet. Only 75 feet of climbing. Moderate.
    This is the most westerly gully. 50 feet of rock scrambling, followed by 150 feet of scree leads to a split

in the gully. The right-hand branch is taken. Climbing starts a further 50 feet above the split.

1) 35 feet. This pitch consists of three chockstones. The first is climbed left, right, or through ; the second over ; the third left. Walk 30 feet.

2) 20 feet. Pass under an archway and climb the right wall to a belay under a big block.

3) 20 feet. Climb in, then out to the top of the block.
   Jack's Rake may be joined on the right above the first pitch.

GREAT GULLY.—330 feet. Difficult. This is the right-hand and longer one of the two deeply-marked gullies towards the western end of the crag. One of the few good gully climbs in the district.

1) 150 feet. 40 feet of easy rocks form a prelude to 110 feet of scrambling, which leads to a cave beneath a huge chockstone.

2) 35 feet. The wall on the right is climbed using a foot-hold on the chockstone. Alternatively the leader may enter the cave and leave by the window.

3) 50 feet. Rock and scree scrambling leads to a small cave.

4) 10 feet. Climb through or over the cave.

5) 65 feet. The Brant and Slape above requires a little care in the choice of holds for the first few feet. A pleasant slab pitch.

6) 20 feet. There are now three alternatives, a very difficult scoop on the left, an easy through route, or an easy grass exit on the right.

A grassy gully a few yards to the right leads with two easy pitches to the summit ; or Jack's Rake, running off to the right, offers an easy descent.

STONY BUTTRESS.—370 feet. Severe. The buttress to the right of Great Gully, between that and the Crescent Climb. Loose rock requires care. A disappointing climb.

After about 60 feet of heathery scrambling a shelf, with belay, is reached on the edge of Great Gully.

(1) 40 feet. Climb diagonally upwards to the right.

(2) 50 feet. Continue upwards to the right until, after rounding a corner and taking a step up, a shelf is reached with belay at the right-hand end.

(3) 40 feet. Climb the obvious steep groove (poor rock) and break out onto steep grass ledges on the left. Belay.

(4) 70 feet. From the belay step a little right, then work back leftwards through the bilberries.

(5) 100 feet. Pastures lead to a belay in a corner.

(6) 70 feet. Climb onto the large rock shelf on the right. A steep little ridge farther right leads to another large shelf and a pleasant arête leads still rightwards to Jack's Rake.

CRESCENT CLIMB.—330 feet. Moderate. The climb starts to the right of Stony Buttress and goes up the broken arête on the immediate right of a shallow, dirt-filled gully. The recent rock-fall from Stony Buttress has rendered the lower section dangerously loose and friable without materially increasing its technical difficulty.

(1) 180 feet. The arête is followed to a ledge with flake above at the left end of the Crescent proper. Stances and doubtful belays *en route*.

(2) 50 feet. A pleasant traverse to the right on large holds under the overhang. Good belay.

(3) 100 feet. The grassy slabs above lead to Jack's Rake.

CRESCENT WALL.—180 feet. Severe. A rather indefinite route on the steep, mossy slabs to the right of the first section of the Crescent Climb. Disappointing, but finishes well. Starts about 50 feet to the right of the Crescent Climb below easy rocks.

(1) 30 feet. Diagonally left to a ledge.

(2) 90 feet. Climb steep rocks of increasing difficulty, still working left, until an obvious grassy traverse leads round to the right to a ledge with flake belay. The pitch may be split by traversing left to the Crescent Climb after 40 feet. The whole of this section is very mossy.

(3) 60 feet. Work diagonally right for a few feet, then continue straight up clean slabs to the Crescent. (It is possible to traverse onto Crescent Slabs from the foot of this pitch.)

CRESCENT SLABS.—200 feet. Severe. A good slab climb taking a roughly parallel course to Crescent Wall. Starts at an obvious weakness at the right-hand end of the slabs which debouch from the Crescent.

(1) 40 feet. A rising gangway to the left. It is usually wet.

(2) 40 feet. Traverse obliquely right into a shallow groove. After a few feet of ascent leave on the left and work over easier slabs to a spike-belay.

Alternatively, and more easily, traverse horizontally left and climb a slab on the left of the second small holly-tree.

(3) 35 feet. Steep slabs with good holds immediately above

the belay lead to a grassy shelf. Belay down on the right under the wall.

(4)　25 feet. An upward traverse to the right leads with difficulty to a small shelf with belay for line.

(5)　60 feet. The pleasant slabs are climbed direct to a belay at the right-hand end of the Crescent Traverse.

WAILING WALL.—200 feet. Very severe. Beyond Crescent Slabs the main, or Central, buttress assumes the steepness of a wall, characterized by an obvious stratum of rock, the Barrier at its foot. The climb roughly follows an obvious corner running up the left-hand side of this steeper section and provides interesting, if not outstanding, climbing. Starts a few feet to the right of Crescent Slabs below an undercut groove.

(1)　10 feet. The Barrier (very low here) is climbed to a stance and belay below the groove.

(2)　15 feet. The groove is very awkward to start (a shoulder may be useful). Poor holds then lead to a small stance and excellent belay.

(3)　40 feet. Traverse to the right into a groove and continue to a gangway running up to the left. This is followed for about 20 feet to its left end, when a stride is made to a grass shelf with large flake-belay.

(4)　90 feet. The shallow corner on the right leads to a small ledge. Continue up a dirty and harder section for a few feet until an exposed traverse can be made to the right for about 20 feet (holly-tree for running belay) to a grassy ledge. A second ledge above and to the right is gained by an awkward movement, when a delightful traverse leads back left into a corner with a good thread-belay.

(5) 45 feet. Starting just to the right of the corner two awkward steps bring better holds within reach. Short, steep walls follow until a ledge is reached at about 30 feet. Traverse left from here into a grassy corner. Belay. 110 feet of scrambling lead to Jack's Rake below Gwynne's Chimney.

ALPH.—275 feet. Very severe. An interesting route of some difficulty following a somewhat tortuous line up the steep face on the right of Wailing Wall. Starts a few feet to the left of Wailing Wall.

(1) 10 feet. Ascend the Barrier.

(2) 25 feet. Ascend the overhang where it is broken by a shallow depression (15 feet left of Pitch 2, Wailing Wall) and traverse horizontally right to the good belay and poor stance on Wailing Wall.

(3) 80 feet. The objective is a small grass ledge and holly-tree away up to the right. It is reached by a diagonal ascent on rather shelving holds. Belay on holly-tree.

(4) 60 feet. Step down to the left and make an awkward move out onto the left wall. Traverse left for a few feet to a shallow groove which is ascended to a small juniper ledge. Traverse left again to a grass ledge, then up to another grass ledge. The rib at the left-hand end of the ledge is climbed for about 10 feet when a horizontal traverse can be made back to the right to a good ledge. Ash-tree belay.

(5) 100 feet. Traverse right along the ledge past a juniper bush to a loose square block below a corner. Climb the corner to the overhang, which is turned on the left, and climb straight up to Jack's Rake about 50 feet higher.

DECEPTION.—185 feet. Severe. A good climb. Difficulties, quite considerable in places, are all well protected. The route follows the easy-looking grassy corner on the immediate right of the central wall up which lies Alph. Starts below the Barrier, a little to the right of the corner.

(1) 20 feet. Climb the Barrier to the ledge below the overhang, then walk left along the ledge to the foot of the groove. Belay.

(2) 75 feet. The groove is climbed to a holly-tree near which is a good spike for a running belay. An awkward step right is then made to grassy rocks which are ascended to a grass ledge in the corner. Poor belay 8 feet higher on left.

(3) 40 feet. Work diagonally right over grass ledges, then straight up to a large ledge at the foot of a slab, overhung on its left. Belay on the slab.

(4) 45 feet. The slab is climbed at its left-hand corner, where it meets a steep wall. A withered holly-tree is attained with difficulty, when a delicate traverse can be made to the right up to a good ledge. A fine thread-belay will be found in the niche above on the left. Jack's Rake is reached a few feet higher on the right.

GWYNNE'S CHIMNEY.—80 feet. Difficult. Quite a pleasant little chimney. Starts from Jack's Rake a few feet to the right of the end of The Crescent to which it can form a pleasant finish.

(1) 55 feet. Climb the chimney direct to the Gun.

(2) 25 feet. Climb the right wall via the crack, or, more pleasantly, step right from the Gun to the arête, then up.

If desired, further climbing can be obtained to the summit either by following the well-scratched route via a steep crack in the little buttress above or by traversing 20 feet right and finishing up the last two pitches of Cook's Tour.

Cook's Tour.—300 feet. Very difficult. The pitches are mainly short and belays good, the route being generally suitable for an inexperienced party. Starts at a cairn on Jack's Rake half-way between Gwynne's Chimney and Rake End Chimney.

1) 20 feet. The open groove leads to a platform and belays.

2) 35 feet. Climb the steep slab ahead and move round to the right onto the top of a pinnacle. Massive belays.

3) 40 feet. From the corner on the left easy climbing is followed by steep bracken leading to a doubtful flake-belay at the foot of an imposing slab.

4) 85 feet. Move up to a large grass ledge 30 feet away on the left and walk along it for 50 feet to a flake-belay below an open grassy gully.

5) 20 feet. Climb the gully and move right to a grass ledge. Pinnacle-belay.

6) 15 feet. Traverse to the right round the outside of the flake, then up to a pleasant grassy corner. Ash-tree belay.

7) 25 feet. The crack behind the tree is ascended to the top of the flake. Higher, on the left, is a corner with flake-belay.

8) 20 feet. The steep slab above is climbed to a good ledge, but poor belay. For this reason it is probably advisable to continue up the next pitch.

(9)   40 feet. The wall is climbed to the top, first slightly right, then straight up. Belay.

BRACKEN ROUTE.—375 feet. Severe in boots. Offers some quite interesting climbing despite the aptness of its name, providing a logical continuation to Deception. Follows Cook's Tour for the first three pitches and then breaks out to the right.

(1), (2) and (3).—As for Cook's Tour.

(4)   90 feet. Climb to the right of the huge, smooth slab for 20 feet, then up to a ledge on the right. The ledge is traversed to its right-hand end when a 15-foot descent leads to a shelf and good belay.

(5)   30 feet. Traverse across the heather to a belay below a corner.

(6)   60 feet. The corner is climbed for 30 feet, when it is possible to step right on to the arête. This is climbed on good, small holds to a good stance and thread-belay in jammed quartz blocks.

(7)   30 feet. A rising traverse to the right to large pinnacle-belay.

(8)   40 feet. The steep face behind the belay provides delicate climbing throughout if done direct. It is possible to work leftwards after 20 feet across to easier ledges.

(9)   30 feet. Easier climbing leads to the top.

RAKE END CHIMNEY.—235 feet. Very difficult. A very good climb of its type, suitable for any weather conditions. Starts, as the name implies, at the foot of Jack's Rake.

(1)   35 feet. Easy grass steps lead to the Chimney proper.

(2)   25 feet. Climb the chimney, facing right, to a ledge and belay in the bed.

3) 20 feet. A repetition of Pitch 2, with a move into the open air in passing, leads to a second ledge and belay.

4) 20 feet. Proceed still up the chimney over a large chock-stone. Useful footholds on the left.

5) 70 feet. A walk up the gully.

6) 15 feet. Climb onto a windowsill.

7) 35 feet. Through the window and up the right wall.

8) 15 feet. A small cave passed on the left. A walk then leads to the summit.

RAKE END WALL.—210 feet. Very severe. An excellent climb on clean rock up the steep wall which bounds Rake End Chimney on the right, only marred by its junction with the Chimney at the end of Pitch 3. The standard of difficulty is well maintained throughout. Starts 15 feet to the right of the Chimney, beyond its bounding rib.

1) 70 feet. Commencing on the right the rib is climbed direct past a good flake and up an ill-defined crack until its steepening necessitates a move round the corner to the right. A diagonal crack is then followed to a huge block below an overhanging corner. Thread-belays with stance on the right.

2) 35 feet. The imposing crack in the corner. It is climbed by the layback method to a bilberry ledge with a thread-belay 10 feet higher.

3) 65 feet. From the lower end of the ledge step round to the left onto a fine slab. After a direct ascent to the right of a slight overhang it is possible to make a delicate move onto the arête on the left. This soon leads to the large grass terrace at the top of Pitch 4 of the Chimney.

F

(4) 40 feet. The last pitch lies up the right-bounding wall
     of the next section of the Chimney. Its start is reached
     by walking 30 feet up the grass. The wall, awkward
     at first, is climbed by its left-hand edge except for a
     detour to the right to avoid the steepest section.

STOATS' CRACK.—375 feet. Severe. An enjoyable climb for the
     cragsman and botanist alike. Starts at the extreme
     right-hand corner of the East Buttress, where it
     bends round into the easy scree gully. The first
     objective is the steep crack formed by a subsidiary
     buttress lying against the main wall.

(1) 30 feet. A vertical grassy corner, usually wet, leading to
     the right-hand end of a long grass shelf. Belay.

(2) 25 feet. Descend a little and walk along the grass to the
     foot of the crack. Belay.

(3) 20 feet. The crack is followed to a belay.

(4) 45 feet. After a few feet in the crack break out to the left
     and ascend to a stance and belay on the corner.

(5) 35 feet. The groove on the left is reached by a short
     traverse and followed to a ledge with belays.

(6) 50 feet. The corner above gives an interesting pitch.
     A capacious, overhung ledge is reached with sapling
     belays.

(7) 80 feet. Step round to the left along the grass terrace
     and climb an open groove (finish to right) ; then
     traverse another grass shelf to the left to an easy
     bilberry-filled groove. This is followed by grass to
     belays. About 15 feet to the right is a small belay below
     a sweep of slabs.

     A more direct route from the top of the open groove lies
     up the wall to the right of the bilberry-filled groove or

small holds. It is harder than any other part of the climb.

8) 50 feet. Pleasant slabs, delicate at first, lead to a ledge and belays.

9) 40 feet. Climb a short wall and follow slabs leftwards to a huge detached block. 100 feet of scrambling finishes the climb.

IOBSON'S CHOICE.—205 feet. Severe. Follows what appears to be the only feasible line up the very steep right-hand wall of the East Buttress and takes the form of an ascending traverse to the left. The chief difficulties and interest are concentrated in the first two pitches. Starts below and to the right of a sweep of slabs reached by scrambling about half-way up the subsidiary left-hand branch of the easy scree gully.

1) 55 feet. Follow a diagonal line leftwards across the slabs until a good flake enables a long stride to be made into a grassy recess below a fair-sized tree. Belay.

2) 40 feet. The slightly impending, fluted wall above and to the left of the belay is awkward to start, but the angle soon eases and a belay is reached in a sloping corner below an impossible groove.

3) 50 feet. Take the easiest line leftwards to the foot of a crack topped by a juniper bush. Climb the crack to a belay on the vegetatious ledge above.

4) 60 feet. Continue the traverse along the ledge until a square chimney provides a route to the top of the crag.

BENNISON'S CHIMNEY and GIBSON'S CHIMNEY are the two final weaknesses of the East Buttress, starting high up the scree gully. The former will be enjoyed only

by the nerveless devotee of vertical grass climbing
the latter is less frightening but offers only 50 fee
of climbing.

RAVEN CRAG

Included under this heading are : the original Raven Crag now referred to as Raven Crag Buttress), Middlefell Buttress n its left, and the line of low crags extending towards the New Hotel—separated from the Buttress by a sweep of screes. The latter are known collectively as the East Crag.

The climbs are described from left to right.

MIDDLEFELL BUTTRESS.—250 feet. Difficult. First pitch very difficult, but can be avoided. Starts at the lowest point of the cleanest looking buttress immediately behind the Old Dungeon Ghyll Hotel and about 10 minutes away from it.

1) 50 feet. A highly polished and rather strenuous crack leads in 40 feet to a platform with large block-belays. An easy alternative to the left of the buttress leads to the same ledge. In 10 feet more a grass terrace is reached.

2) 150 feet. The second section of only moderate climbing follows the scratches along the left side of the buttress to a second grass terrace. Belays are good and frequent.

3) 50 feet. Start the wall above rather to the right, traverse 10 feet to the left, then up a fairly steep section to the finishing balcony.

An additional pitch can be obtained by the ascent of a short, but steep slab (Curtain Wall) some distance higher on the right.

RAVEN CRAG BUTTRESS is separated from Middlefell Buttress by an open gully (Raven Gully) and is bounded on its right by the Amphitheatre. It is steep, particularly in the centre

where there is an impenetrable line of overhangs, and somewha
vegetatious. The rock is good, however, and there is a
interesting selection of climbs, some of them considerabl
exposed in their upper section.

A rapid means of descent is afforded by a large grass she
(Oak-tree Terrace) which gives easy access to the Amphitheatr
from the upper-right-hand section of the Crag. The terrace i
reached from the top by a short descent over some large spli
blocks (the final pitch of Savernake). Raven Gully is a
alternative way down but is rather awkward if wet.

EVENING WALL.—155 feet. Severe. Starts from Raven Gull
        about 20 feet to the left of the pinnacle belay at the to
        of the first pitch of Oak-tree Wall.

(1)   35 feet. From the cairn ascend for 15 feet until the wal
        steepens when a traverse right is made into a heather
        corner. Step right and move up to a small stance an
        belay on the second pitch of Oak-tree Wall.

(2)   30 feet. Ascend 10 feet to a ledge, traverse left and ther
        go straight up to a bulge. Small spike-belay.

(3)   20 feet. Step up from the belay and traverse left via a
        awkward corner to an ash-tree. Belay.

(4)   70 feet. An arête on the right is attained by an awkward
        move and ascended to the top on good holds.

OAK-TREE WALL.—135 feet. Severe. Of a similar standard to
        the Original Route, perhaps a little easier. Starts to the
        left of and 40 feet higher than the Original Route
        just below a prominent oak-tree.

(1)   45 feet. A short crack is climbed to the roots of the oak
        tree when a move out on to the right wall is made
        followed by an ascent to a small ledge. Continue

upwards to a larger ledge with a pinnacle belay at its left-hand end.

(2) 45 feet. The rib immediately behind the belay is followed to a small ledge below a bulging wall. An overhung gangway leads up to the right to a small stance on the Original Route. Spike-belay (for line, only) a few feet higher.

(3) 45 feet. Ascend slightly right, bearing away from the Original Route on the left, to a ledge below a bulge. Then up to the bulge and turn it on its left by way of a shallow scoop.

THE ORIGINAL ROUTE.—200 feet. Severe. A pleasant and well-marked route. Starts at the lowest point of the left-hand section of the Buttress.

(1) 40 feet. Ascend slightly left up a miniature gully to a ledge and belay.

(2) 50 feet. A steep ridge ahead leads to a heather shelf which is traversed to the left for about 30 feet to the large pinnacle belay on Oak-tree Wall.

(3) 45 feet. Move a few feet back to the right and climb the steep wall above, veering slightly right to a group of ledges. To the left of the topmost ledge will be found a small but good belay.

(4) 65 feet. Straight ahead for 15 feet, then a pleasant movement left to a belayless ledge and straight on again to the finish on the fell. The last 20 feet are steep with small holds.

HOLLY-TREE TRAVERSE.—170 feet. Very difficult. An interesting, if somewhat rambling route. Starts from Raven Gully a little lower than the start of Evening Wall.

(1) 20 feet. Scramble up to the pinnacle-belay at the foot of Pitch 2, Oak-tree Wall.

(2) 45 feet. The ridge above the belay is followed for about 10 feet until it is possible to make a rather awkward traverse right to a sentry box and belay on the Original Route.

(3) 30 feet. Continue the traverse to the right, making for a conspicuous holly-tree. Belay round tree.

(4) 45 feet. Climb the wall to the right of the gully to a rock ledge below a right-angled corner.

(5) 30 feet. Climb the right-angled corner on good holds to the finish.

VARIATION FINISH

(4a) 20 feet. From the holly-tree climb the gully to a small oak-tree.

(5a) 70 feet. Leave the gully for the arête to the left which is climbed working slightly to the left to the finish.

BILBERRY BUTTRESS.—255 feet. Very severe. A climb with a well-maintained standard of difficulty and a fine, airy finish. Starts at a cairn at the lowest point of the right-hand side of the crag.

(1) 25 feet. Easy rocks to the foot of a crack. Belay.

(2) 40 feet. The crack is climbed with some difficulty and is followed by easier climbing slightly left to a grass ledge and massive flake-belays.

(3) 55 feet. A thin crack in the steep wall above is climbed to a bulge which is surmounted with the aid of small, sharp handholds and a magnificent finishing hold. The ridge on the left is then followed to a large, but sloping, bilberry ledge. Belay at point of arrival for sitting position, only.

(4) 80 feet. A vegetatious pitch on rather doubtful rock. The ledge is traversed to the right to a mossy crack. This is climbed for a few feet, followed by a short traverse left beneath a large, detached mass of rock to a scoop. Oak-tree-belay at top of scoop.

(5) 55 feet. Descend as far as the doubtful block and then traverse diagonally down to the left beneath the overhang. Continue horizontally until a groove is reached. An exit is made to the left after an upward step and the top attained without further difficulty. Belay above the middle of the traverse. The last two pitches can be combined, thus avoiding the visit to the oak-tree.

SAVERNAKE.—255 feet. Severe. Follows a similar general line to Bilberry Buttress but is more circuitous and a great deal easier. Start at the same point as Bilberry Buttress.

(1) 25 feet. The first pitch of Bilberry Butress. Easy rocks to the foot of the crack.

(2) 60 feet. Step down and round the corner on the right and then up the easy V-chimney to the top of Pitch 2, Bilberry Buttress.

(3) 70 feet. Walk down to the left and then up the broken rocks in the corner which gradually steepen to a good finish at the top of Pitch 3, Bilberry Buttress.

(4) 50 feet. Traverse the sloping ledge to the right-hand end and climb the broken corner until a step left can be made into a dirty scoop. Then climb up over the large detached block and follow broken rocks to the right to a large ledge and fine oak-tree belay.

(5) 50 feet. Walk round to the right and climb over the large blocks to the finish.

REVELATION.—165 feet. Severe. A pleasant route providing steep climbing on small, but adequate holds. Starts at the foot of the right-hand face of the crag 15 feet to the right of a holly-tree and follows a prominent buttress bounded on the right in its upper section by an open chimney.

(1)   40 feet. Straight up the buttress on small holds to a good ledge and belay below an overhanging wall.

(2)   50 feet. The wall above is overcome by means of a short, but strenuous crack. The angle eases a little and a small grass ledge is reached. (Running belay low down on right.) This point can also be reached by a short traverse right followed by an upward traverse back left to avoid the overhanging crack. This was the route originally followed. Continue up the face from the grass ledge and over a projecting nose to a sloping stance and good belay. Kneewrecker Chimney is immediately on the right.

(3)   50 feet. Continue straight up over bulging rocks to the Oak-tree Terrace. Belay at back of Terrace on the tree.

(4)   25 feet. Finish behind the split blocks as for Savernake. Alternatively, the route can be extended, as in the original ascent by reversing the last two pitches of the Girdle Traverse.

(4a) 40 feet. Traverse behind the large blocks and continue to the left along a ledge. Descend slightly and then move up to a good rock ledge. A stance is taken just above the ledge with a belay in the crack behind a tuft of grass. (Pitch 6, Girdle Traverse, reversed.)

(5a) 40 feet. Climb down to the left on good holds to a steep groove, up this for a few feet and then traverse upwards to finish over the corner to the left. (Pitch 5, Girdle Traverse, reversed.)

KNEEWRECKER CHIMNEY.—125 feet. Very severe. A strenuous climb, the hardest on the Crag. Follows the open chimney on the right of Revelation starting from the oak-tree a short way to the right of the second pitch of that climb.

(1)   40 feet. The wall on the left of the tree is ascended until an entry can be made into an open scoop which is followed to a sloping ledge and good belay on the left. (Top of Pitch 2, Revelation.)

(2)   50 feet. Step back to the right and climb a strenuous, overhanging crack facing first right and then left. The rock is lichenous, particularly near the top. Oak-tree Terrace is reached and followed to the tree belay.

(3)   35 feet. The overhanging V-chimney immediately behind the oak-tree is climbed facing right for about 20 feet to a standing position on a tiny ledge, rather painful use being made of the right knee in the attainment of this objective. The overhang becomes more pronounced and after an upward step an escape is made on to good holds round the corner on the left which give easy access to the top.

RAVEN GIRDLE.—290 feet. Severe. Traverses the buttress from left to right, providing pleasant climbing and airy situations.

(1)   35 feet. Pitch 1, Evening Wall.

(2)   40 feet. Continue up Pitch 2 of Oak-tree Wall to the small belay at the end of the gangway.

(3) 80 feet. Traverse right, making for the prominent rock ledge on the skyline. The first 10 feet is a semi-hand-traverse under the overhang with an awkward move at the end. After crossing a small gully it is best to ascend slightly and then descend to the rock ledge. Continue the descent to a gnarled tree (above the holly-tree of Holly-tree Traverse) and cross the wall on the right to a ledge below a right-angled corner. Top of Pitch 4, Holly-tree Traverse.

(4) 35 feet. Climb down over two massive and doubtful-looking blocks to a delightfully exposed slab which is traversed to the right to a ledge and belay.

(5) 40 feet. Descend a little and traverse right to an incipient gully, down again for a few feet and continue the traverse up to the right to a rock ledge. Stance and belay just above the ledge. This pitch is exposed but not particularly difficult.

(6) 40 feet. Continue the traverse to Oak-tree Terrace.

(7) 20 feet. Finish behind the split blocks as for Savernake. Bounding the Buttress high on its right is a grassy basin (the Amphitheatre) the walls of which provide the following three climbs.

BLUEBELL GULLY.—150 feet. Severe. An open grassy gully to the left of a prominent rock pinnacle. The climbing is better than the appearance suggests.

(1) 50 feet. Climb up the gully past a small rowan-tree to a grassy corner (The Window Box). Belay round holly-tree.

(2) 55 feet. Continue up the gully for about 6 feet until a rather awkward traverse can be made to the right on

to a steep wall which is climbed to a ledge. Small belay, suitable for line only.

(3) 45 feet. Ascend above the belay on small holds until it is possible to make an awkward step into the gully on the left and continue up it to the top.

BLUEBELL ARÊTE.—145 feet. Severe. Starts 10 feet to the right of Bluebell Gully and follows the steep arête between that climb and Centipede.

(1) 50 feet. Climb into a groove on the right below a small rowan-tree and ascend for a few feet until it is possible to climb the steep right wall to the level of the tree, when a traverse left is made to the arête proper. Climb the arête to a small stance and tree-belay.

(2) 50 feet. Continue up the steep edge of the arête, the first few feet and the final moves being the hardest.

(3) 45 feet. Finish up the last pitch of Bluebell Gully.

CENTIPEDE.—300 feet. Severe. A very pleasant route. Starts at a cairn to the right of and lower than Bluebell Gully below the prominent pinnacle.

(1) 60 feet. Climb the steep rib until a traverse can be made to the left to a crack which leads to a good ledge.

(2) 50 feet. Climb the steep slabs to the overhang, then traverse left round the corner below the overhang and climb up the gully to a stance below a crack on the right wall. Good thread-belay.

(3) 50 feet. Step down a few feet and traverse to the right across the wall to join the arête at a small rock ledge immediately above the overhang. Climb straight up

the arête to a good ledge. Good belay high up on the start of the next pitch.

(4) 55 feet. The steep wall ahead is climbed direct. The first few feet are the hardest. A pull-up over a flake is followed by pleasant climbing to a ledge.

(5) 70 feet. Continue up the next step on the ridge, which is more awkward than it looks, to another good ledge.

(6) 15 feet. Easier climbing to the finish.

STEWPOT.—110 feet. Severe (last pitch only). This climb is situated on the small broken-looking buttress some 100 yards to the right of the Amphitheatre. Starts at the lowest point of the buttress.

(1) 40 feet. Climb up broken rocks to a large detached block. Climb over the block and continue up a slab to a ledge with another detached rock.

(2) 35 feet. A small slab is climbed, followed by broken rocks upwards and to the right, then slightly left to a rock ledge with a large pinnacle on the left. Belay in the crack.

(3) 35 feet. Climb onto the pinnacle and finish up the wall to the right. The finishing move is very awkward and is much harder than the rest of the climb.

The East Crag.

THE EAST CRAG is the name given to a line of small, but very steep buttresses extending from Raven Crag Buttress towards the New Hotel. They have received little attention up to the present, probably due to their uncompromising appearance.

BASKERVILLE.—100 feet. Very severe. About half-way along the first line of crags is a deep-cut right-angled corner containing a large holly-tree. Baskerville lies up the steep rib on its immediate left and gives a single pitch of which the lower half is continuously severe.

(1) 100 feet. A small rock ledge about 20 feet up is attained either directly by the ascent of a groove or by traversing in from about 20 feet to the left. Both are of about the same order of difficulty. The edge on the right is then followed to the top, the major difficulty being the surmounting of a bulge at about 35 feet. The upper section consists of an easy-angled ridge.

WATSON WALL.—100 feet. Severe. The route lies up the wall about 50 yards to the right of Baskerville and is readily recognised by the 2-foot overhang about 15 feet up.

(1) 100 feet. The overhang is surmounted by means of an awkward mantelshelf when a short traverse left can be made into a shallow niche. A diagonal ascent is then made to the right to a small ledge on the rib. The pitch can be split here, if desired, by using a rather doubtful spike-belay (for line only) about 10 feet above the ledge. The rib is then followed for about 15 feet when a traverse left is made onto the face which is climbed to the top.

Some two or three hundred yards nearer to the New Hotel and lower down the fellside is another short, steep buttress.

PIANISSIMO.—75 feet. Severe. The arête on the extreme right of the crag. Starts to the right of a holly-tree.

(1) 25 feet. Climb up to and through the tree. Belay on left.

(2) 50 feet. Traverse right on small holds to the arête and

attain a small ledge by means of a mantelshelf. Again
right and then diagonally left up the corner to finish
up broken rocks.

The following climb on the same crag is described by
W. Peascod in the 1947 Journal of the Fell and Rock
Climbing Club.

Standard : Very difficult, excepting Pitch (4) which is
very severe in boots. 130 feet. Starts at the lowest
point of the crag on the right-hand side beneath some
bulging, lichen-covered rocks.

(1) 30 feet. Straight up to the higher of two rock ledges
under a large bulge. Small spike-belays on left.

(2) 30 feet. Work round the nose on the right and pull up
onto a sloping rock ledge using good holds high up.
Continue up to spike-belays.

(3) 30 feet. Up the rocks above the belay to a large triangular
grass ledge with steep walls on two sides. A slightly
overhanging crack runs up the junction of the two
walls. Belay near foot of crack.

(4) 25 feet. The crack is climbed on poor holds and is
strenuous. About 15 feet up a bracket on the right
wall gives good holds for the pull-up onto a small
ledge. Ascend higher until stopped by a large overhang. Small ledge and belay beneath overhang.

(5) 15 feet. Traverse left under the overhang on good flake
holds to a small slab which is followed to the top.

BOWFELL

THE APPROACHES

LANGDALE.—The climbs on Bowfell are most comfortably reached from Langdale by way of the Three Tarns track leading up The Band. The track keeps to the left of the ridge and overlooks Oxendale and Hell Ghyll. After the fairly steep preliminary section The Band levels out rather and the track veers to the right, passing above Neckband crag on the Mickleden side. When the ridge running up to Bowfell is reached, the track, which now turns left, is quitted and one ascends the ridge itself until a cairn on a patch of red scree indicates the next turning. From here an undulating trod, reminiscent of the High Level Route to Pillar Rock leads to the right below a line of outcrops, passes underneath Flat Crags and the Cambridge Crag, and drops over a scree-shoot to the foot of Bowfell Buttress.

The Buttress can be reached from Mickleden either by taking a diagonal line up Green Tongue, which is about halfway up the valley, or by ascending the first section of Rossett Ghyll and then working back leftwards over rough ground straight for the Crag. The Band route will be thought easier.

WASDALE.—Bowfell is within reasonable walking distance of Wasdale (2 to 2½ hours). The route goes up Sty Head and Esk Hause and over Esk Pike to the top of Bowfell Buttress.

BORROWDALE.—From this valley walk up Langstrath and Stake Pass and over Rossett Crag to arrive at the top of Rossett Ghyll. From here a diagonal route, keeping to the left of Hanging Knott, leads to the summit of Bowfell.

G

Topographical

The main climbs on Bowfell are situated on three separate crags in a rough semi-circle towards the summit of the mountain. They are supplemented by recent additions on the lower and smaller Neckband Crag. Of the three upper crags the first reached from Langdale is Flat Crags, facing almost due north, and easily recognisable from its name. The rock is of a peculiar formation, consisting of steep, smooth walls separated by a series of flat gangways running upwards from right to left, the topmost one leading easily to the main ridge.

From the right-hand end of this highest gangway rises the Cambridge Crag, facing north-east, and, like both Flat Crags and Bowfell Buttress, having a sharp-cut obtuse-angled base. The rock formation is entirely different from Flat Crags and consists of numerous sharp-topped broken ridges, separated by short grooves and cracks.

Beyond this crag comes a wide fan-shaped scree-shoot running down from the main ridge and then, facing east, the imposing Bowfell Buttress. The Buttress has a well-marked nose dividing it definitely into two different faces. On the left the end-on strata form ridges and cracks similar to the Cambridge Crag, and here lie most of its climbs. On the right the cleavage face offers an almost unbroken slab, from top to bottom.

The crag appears from below to lie against the fell-side. In actual fact it is cut off behind by a cleft which runs south over broken rock and scree into the fan-shaped scree-shoot from the main ridge to give an easy means of descent, and north to join the steep gully which bounds the Buttress on its northern side. This gully (North Gully) contains a steep pitch near the bottom, but it can be entered from below either by an excursion up the fell-side on the right, or by moderate climbing up the corner of the buttress for 80 feet, followed by a difficult 15-foot wall to the level of a niche of blocks, when a traverse to the right leads in just above the pitch.

The Climbs

FLAT CRAGS CLIMB.—150 feet. Severe. A cairn at the right-hand and lower end of a large rock gangway marks the start. The climb can be abandoned by walking to the right from any stance.

(1) 45 feet. Climb direct up a steep slab on smooth holds, stepping left to a recess at 20 feet. Traverse right and upwards to a good ledge. A small belay can be lassoed on the wall 10 feet above, or a flake utilised just below the ledge. There is also a thread-belay.

(2) 55 feet. Traverse left along the ledge for 20 feet round an awkward corner where holds are small, then to a large terrace with belays.

(3) 35 feet. A steep chimney lies ahead. This is entered via a groove on the left (belay 10 feet above terrace), followed by a difficult step to the right. Holds in the chimney are small.

(4) 15 feet. A smooth slab on the left gives a rock finish to a somewhat artificial climb.

BORSTAL BUTTRESS.—230 feet. Severe. This is situated on the Cambridge Crag. The start is to the left of a steep wall in a corner about 60 paces above and to the left of the Waterspout. The first pitch is good but the succeeding ones can all be avoided on grass.

(1) 75 feet. Traverse right across the wall, then straight up,

The final section up a steep V-chimney requires care due to loose holds near the finish. Belay.

(2) 45 feet. Climb the rib on the right and cross a slab, via a crack running to the right, to a crevasse and boulders.

(3) 65 feet. Steep grass leads to the left by several small chimneys, the last loose one of which may be avoided on the right. Belay.

(4) 25 feet. Cross the rib on the right and descend into a V-corner. Belay high on the right wall.

(5) 20 feet. A thin groove running up to the left, with few holds and a little grass, is followed by scrambling to the top.

THE CAMBRIDGE CLIMB.—250 feet. Difficult. An interesting route which can be awkward under wet conditions. Starts at a cairn just to the left of the Waterspout at the foot of a broad slab sloping upwards to the right.

(1) 35 feet. Climb the slab to a corner with thread-belay.

(2) 30 feet. Step round the corner to the right and then ascend on good holds to a ledge with overhanging block-belay.

(3) 20 feet. Traverse left to the second of two grass nooks.

(4) 25 feet. A sharp jutting flake above is passed to attain a grassy corner and belay.

(5) 50 feet. A pleasant chimney, finishing on a grass shelf with a large embedded spike-belay to the right.

(6) 35 feet. The steep wall behind the belay leads back into the chimney, though an easier entry can be made at the level of the belay shelf. Then ascend to a large terrace.

(7) 55 feet. A large scale three-step staircase leads upwards to the right to the finishing balcony.

Easy scrambling up the dirty gully on the right brings one
onto the main ridge.

Bowfell Buttress

THE PLAQUE ROUTE.—280 feet. Very difficult. A pleasant
all-weather climb, fitted with good belays, up the
left-hand edge of Bowfell Buttress. Starts from a
large boulder belay at the point where scree and a
grass terrace meet at the foot of the crag.

(1) 40 feet. Straight up past a shelf at 10 feet followed by a
very difficult crack or an easier scoop to the left and
then easy rocks to a good belay.

(2) 40 feet. Climb the rib above, which has a crack on its
right, to a small stance and belay.

(3) 40 feet. A mossy groove ahead is followed by a grass
terrace to a belay.

(4) 30 feet. Ascend slabs diagonally to the right on goodholds
to a shelf and belay.

(5) 45 feet. Traverse right into a chimney and then up.
The left wall is formed by a huge detached flake.

(6) 25 feet. Step onto the ridge on the right (where the
Plaque is to be seen) and then up.

(7) 60 feet. Move right over easy slabs and into a chimney
which gives access to the top.

SINISTER SLABS.—345 feet. Very severe. Starts below a rib
about 20 feet to the left of the cairn which marks the
start of the ordinary route. It is one of the easier
climbs of its class, the third pitch being the most
difficult section.

(1) 85 feet. Climb the rib for about 30 feet when a move-

ment is made to the right and over a block. Work
back to the left for 12 feet and then straight up to a
grass shelf and belay.

(2) 25 feet. Climb the slanting grassy chimney on the left
to a good seat with excellent belay below an overhanging corner.

(3) 25 feet. From the corner ascend a narrowing slab slanting
up to the left using small but good fingerholds.
Balance is rather awkward. A poor stance on doubtful
blocks is reached and two small belays.

(4) 30 feet. Climb up over the belays and after a few feet
work over to the right to another poor stance with a
good notch-belay on the rib on the left.

(5) 40 feet. After a step or two on the rib traverse right into
a groove or chimney. After one awkward step good
holds lead to a ledge on the right. Step across to a
good ledge with a belay on the left.

(6) 25 feet. A chimney is entered and followed to a good
stance. Block-belay.

(7) 55 feet. A grassy gully followed by a rib. Block-belay.

(8) 45 feet. After a few feet of easy rocks a crack in the steep
rough slab leads to a flat ledge and belay.

(9) 15 feet. The little wall above lands one at the cairn at
the top of the ordinary route.

THE CENTRAL ROUTE.—255 feet. Severe. An interesting
route of considerable difficulty. Starts 10 feet to the
right of the ordinary route, crosses this at the top of
the first pitch, and thereafter keeps to its left.

(1) 45 feet. Climb the broken groove to the belay below
pitch 2 of Bowfell Buttress route.

(2) 30 feet. The overhanging chimney above is climbed.

The jammed flakes are quite sound and provide excellent holds. Belay above a grass ledge.

(3) 25 feet. The easier continuation of the chimney. Block-belay and another to the right a little higher.

(4) 65 feet. Step left from the rock platform and follow the best line of holds—left again, back right, up and right again to finish. Belay.

(5) 35 feet. Step onto a large block just above the belay to enter a thin groove which is followed with increasing difficulty. The final awkward movement gives entry to a grassy recess with small belay high up on the right.

(6) 15 feet. Climb the steep right corner and cross the rib to a crevassed shelf and belay.

(7) 15 feet. Step back to the left and follow a thin rib to grass shelves and belays.

(8) 25 feet. Follow the slanting slab a few yards on the left to a terrace whence scrambling leads to the top.

BOWFELL BUTTRESS ROUTE.—350 feet. Difficult. A classic route of considerable quality and interest. Starts at a cairn below a ridge slightly to the left of the lowest point of the crag.

(1) 45 feet. The ridge leads to a good belay.

(2) 30 feet. A 12-foot chimney on the right, followed by easy climbing, leads to a rock ledge on a large grass terrace. Small belay.

There is a direct and very difficult start at a small cairn round the corner to the right of the ordinary start.

45 feet. Climb steep slabs finishing by a mossy groove to the right. Large grass terrace and belay.

A walk of 20 feet up to the left brings one to the foot
of pitch 3.

(3) 40 feet. Climb the steep wall above, moving diagonally
up to the left, to a sentry-box in a chimney.   Large
belay.

(4) 60 feet. Follow the chimney for 40 feet (belay) and then
easy ledges to a grass terrace sloping down to the right.
Small belay above. Walk to the right along the
terrace for 25 feet to a crack containing a small belay.

(5) 55 feet. Climb the crack for 15 feet (awkward), then up
to the left via an awkward step to slabby rocks leading
to a pinnacle-belay.

(6) 40 feet. Move left for a few feet and then up a sloping
groove leading into a chimney. Continue to a sloping
slab with flake-belay.

(7) 20 feet. Climb the wall above, whence a long stride to
the left leads upwards to a platform and monumental
belay.

(8) 30 feet. Step back to the right into a grassy groove
leading to a ledge and belay.

(9) 30 feet. Continue up the groove by its left branch to
the finish.

LEDGE AND GROOVE.—335 feet. Very difficult. A rather
rambling route on the edge of the crag overlooking
the North Gully. The latter can be reached from
several points of the climb by easy scrambling to the
right. Starts at a cairn about 100 feet to the right of
the ordinary route and about 15 feet to the left of the
Gully.

(1) 15 feet. A short wall and a groove lead to a large ledge
and belay.

2) 40 feet. Up the rib to a grass ledge which is followed to its right-hand end. Belay.

3) 30 feet. A short wall is followed by a staircase to the right to a ledge below a small overhang.

4) 40 feet. A line of good holds leads up to the left for about 15 feet and then back right to a stance and belay overlooking the Gully.

5) 40 feet. A step up is followed by a traverse to the right to a groove which is ascended for 10 feet to a sloping ledge. The ledge is traversed to the left back to the ridge which is ascended to stance and belay.

6) 25 feet. This is the hardest pitch and is bordering on severe. A delicate traverse is made to the right to a small stance with a good flake-belay 8 feet higher.

7) 25 feet. Traverse right into the chimney and ascend to ledge and large belay.

(8) 25 feet. A groove on the right is followed to a small grass ledge. Rather awkward landing.

(9) 20 feet. Traverse left without difficulty to a belay at the foot of a steep crack.

(10) 20 feet. The crack is climbed for a few feet until an awkward movement can be made onto a small ledge on the left followed by a short, but rather difficult ascent past a projecting block to a large grassy terrace.

(11) 55 feet. Ascend diagonally left into a crack which is followed to a ledge below a 15-foot wall, the ascent of which completes the climb. The final three pitches correspond with pitches 2, 3 and 4 of Right-Hand Wall Traverse.

RIGHT-HAND WALL.—200 feet. Very severe. An interesting route up the steep left-bounding wall of North Gully.

It is considerably exposed in its middle section. Start just above the only pitch in the Gully, at the foot of conspicuous steep corner.

(1) 70 feet. The corner is climbed on good holds to a grass terrace. Block-belay. The Gully can be reached from here by a short walk to the right.

(2) 70 feet. Traverse left across the wall on good flakes then up a short crack to a ledge. The next few feet diagonally left up the wall, are delicate at first but another small ledge is soon gained. A thin groove bearing right from here, is ascended with some difficulty for 15 feet when good holds lead up to a grass ledge and large belay.

(3) 40 feet. Starting a few feet to the right of the belay follow a crack to a grassy terrace.

(4) 20 feet. Another short crack straight ahead leads to the top of the low man.

RIGHT-HAND WALL TRAVERSE.—155 feet. Very difficult. Traverses the left-bounding wall of the Gully from right to left starting at a cairn about two-thirds of the way up the Gully below a series of grass ledges. The major part of the climb is incorporated in the Ledge and Groove.

(1) 45 feet. Follow the broken and grassy rocks slanting up to the left to a conspicuous grass ledge and block-belay.

(2) 20 feet. Traverse left without difficulty to a belay at the foot of a steep crack.

(3) 20 feet. The crack is climbed for a few feet until an awkward movement can be made onto a small ledge on the left followed by a short, but rather difficult ascent past a projecting block to a large grassy terrace.

feet. The face above can be climbed straight up, and is severe. Alternatively, a diagonal ascent is made to the left into a crack which is followed to a ledge below a short wall. This is climbed without difficulty to the top.

CORNER.—140 feet. Just severe. From particulars supplied by R. D. Stevens. Between Right-Hand Wall Traverse and Grey Rib is a corner. The route takes the easiest line up the corner. Grey Rib shows a smooth 20-foot slab to the left. The route starts up this at the foot of the groove.

feet. Climb the groove and mantelshelf to the right onto a square ledge.

feet. Start above the belay for a few feet, then ascent diagonally left to a large block. An ascending traverse right for 10 feet leads to the corner which is ascended to a grass ledge. Traverse 10 feet left to a good belay and moderate stance.

feet. Regain the ledge and ascend the rocky staircase left to a large block. Traverse right and slightly up to a large spike-belay.

feet. Straight up to the top of the buttress.

RIB.—160 feet. Severe. From particulars supplied by R. D. Stevens. The obvious rib which limits the wall 40 feet or so higher up the North Gully than the start of Right-Hand Wall Traverse. A good clean climb.

feet. From the foot of the rib pull up onto the ledge. Large block-belay.

feet. Step right, make an awkward mantelshelf movement, then straight up.

(3) 25 feet. The crest of the rib is followed to a goo

(4) 50 feet. The continuation of the rib is awkward
     but the difficulty eases after 20 feet.

(5) 40 feet. Straight up easily to the top of the butt

BOWFELL BUTTRESS GIRDLE.—The following descrip
     taken from the *Journal of the Fell & Rock C
     Club* :—
         460 feet. Severe. A very interesting climb. Si
         the first pitch of the Plaque Route at the left-ha
         of the face.

(1), (2), (3). The first three pitches of Plaque Route.
     40 feet and 40 feet.

(4) 12 feet. Traverse horizontally right to a grass
     and belay.

(5) 40 feet. A delightful traverse right is made, horiz
     at first, then obliquely upwards, finishing with a
     awkward step round the corner. Belay. (Ju
     with Sinister Slabs.)

(6) 70 feet. Traverse horizontally right to a crevasse
     great nose of the buttress. After a direct asce
     20 feet the traverse is continued, delicately,
     right. Belay.

(7) 50 feet. The short wall above is climbed diag
     from left to right. Belay. (A few feet highel
     ledge to the left, is the pinnacle-belay on the Or
     Route.)

(8) 40 feet. Pitch 6. Ordinary Route, to the flake-bel

(9) 70 feet. A descending traverse is made to the right
     foot of a groove. A very awkward step round
     right follows onto the face of a steep slab. (T
     a small spike on the slab for a loop of line.) A

slight ascent the traverse is continued until a descent
can be made to a grass ledge on the corner of the
buttress.

feet. Traverse round the corner and ascend the steep
wall upwards and to the right. Large platform at the
top of a mossy gully.

is possible to walk off here or a finish can be made up
the last two pitches of Right-Hand Wall.

AND CRAG.—This is the small crag just below the
summit of the Band on the north-east side and the
ascent of the Band followed by a descent to the foot
of the crag forms the easiest means of approach.

he climbs are described from right to left.

1, RIGHT-HAND WALL.—65 feet. Very severe. A
single-pitch climb up the steep little wall at right-
angles to the main mass of the crag.

limb straight up on small holds for 35 feet to the level
of the top of a boss, make an awkward move to the
right, and continue direct to the top.

NECKBAND.—205 feet. Very difficult. A well-marked
route up the prominent rib at the right-hand end of the
crag. A cairn marks the start.

5 feet. Step left from the scree and up into a grassy
groove. The groove may be climbed direct, or an
awkward step taken to the rib on the right. A slab
then leads to a grassy platform with a good belay on
the left.

0 feet. Climb the rib on the right, crossing a broad

ledge and a miniature overhang, and finishi
groove with belays to the left and the right.

(3) 55 feet. Continue up a series of large ledges an
slabs.

(4) 35 feet. Rough rocks straight ahead.

(5) 20 feet. A steep corner on the extreme right, f
by scrambling, leads to the top.

NECTAR.—230 feet. Very severe. After a hard sta
culties rapidly diminish. Starts at a cairn 40
the left of the Neckband Route.

(1) 65 feet. A steep slab is ascended on small hold
few feet until an awkward move can be made
right into an open groove. Ascend direct to a
which is climbed on good holds to a stance and
belay.

(2) 45 feet. Traverse left for 15 feet and climb a p
arête to a grass ledge. Block-belay.

(3) 45 feet. Ascent the short slab on the left and then
crack to a stance and spike-belay.

(4) 35 feet. Climb the easy ridge to a grass ledge.

(5) 40 feet. Straight ahead to the top.

THE GIZZARD.—From particulars supplied by K. H
170 feet. Very severe. Starts at the foot of a
directly beneath a large overhang.

(1) 40 feet. Shattered blocks lead to the start of the
A few feet higher a slight overhang is overcom
difficulty to attain a narrow sentry-box from
easier climbing leads to a ledge and spike-belay

(2) 30 feet. Climb the crack to stance and belay benea
overhang.

3) 40 feet. Traverse horizontally left for 25 feet to a steep corner ; the initial move being delicate. A running-belay can be arranged for the ascent of the corner to a large ledge and belay.

4) 60 feet. Move left along the ledge for 10 feet and climb the steep wall direct on small holds. After 15 feet the climbing becomes easier and is continued to a large ledge and block-belay. Easy rocks give access to the top.

THE GIRDLE TRAVERSE.—200 feet. Very severe. Girdles the crag from right to left, difficulty increasing towards the finish.

1) 35 feet. The first pitch of the Neckband.

2) 50 feet. Pitch 2, Nectar—a short traverse left followed by the ascent of the arête.

3) 35 feet. Traverse left along the ledge. Spike-belay 10 feet higher.

4) 25 feet. An awkward traverse is made to the left round a nose. Block-belay.

5) 55 feet. Continue left along the ledge for 15 feet to a thin crack which contains a piton for use as a running belay. The traverse is completed either by means of a semi-hand-traverse beneath the big overhang or by a very delicate route across the wall above it. Either way provides the hardest climbing on the Traverse. Belays.

From the finish a grass terrace continues round to the left and provides a useful way off.

BOWFELL LINKS.—The Links lie on the Eskdale side of Bowfell just above Three Tarns. There are twelve short chimneys or gullies, mostly of the chockstone variety, but the rock is poor, uninteresting and liberally provided with scree. Commencing from the south end the following climbs may be done :—

(1) A short chimney starting fairly high on the right of an open gully (moderate).

(2) The same gully (left side) with a 35-foot vertical pitch over chockstones (moderate).

(3) A series of four chocks, in all 100 feet (moderate).

(4) The right-hand branch of an open gully ; a grooved wall of about 40 feet (difficult).

(5) The left-hand branch of the same gully ; a vertical pitch crowned by an overhanging chockstone, with a 40-foot finish on the right wall (very difficult).

(6) A chockstone pitch in a scree gully ; ascend on the right wall (very difficult).

Now pass by an all-scree gully.

(7) A scree gully with an overhanging chockstone, 15 feet (difficult).

(8) A grass and scree gully with a 20-foot window pitch (moderate).

(9) A broad scree gully with 10 feet of easy rocks.

(10) 35 feet of scoop and a crack on a buttress.

(11) A 45-foot semi-chimney or crack, with a pull over onto a square flat-topped overhang ; then up the right wall (difficult).

(12) A final crack of 40 feet (severe).

MINOR CRAGS

Scout Crag

An easily accessible crag suitable for any weather conditions ⁓ing low down on the fell beyond the base of White Ghyll, ⁓me quarter-hour's diagonal walking from the New Hotel. ⁓larked by a round top, a few holly bushes and small oaks, it ⁓ossesses six recognised climbs and a variety of short problems. The climbs are described from right to left.

⁓AMBLERS' HANGOVER.—135 feet. Very Difficult. An entertaining climb. Starts at a cairn below a short overhang (usually wet) near the toe of the crag, some 50 feet right of the well-marked start of Route I.

1) 40 feet. The overhang or the easier chimney on its right is followed by 30 feet of slabs leading to a broad grass ledge. Belay.

2) 30 feet. The diamond-shaped wall is climbed to a ledge. From here ascend the bulge ahead to belays.

3) 15 feet. Traverse left to a belay in a grassy recess at the foot of a scoop.

4) 20 feet. Work diagonally right up the groove to an overhang. This is surmounted on good holds to reach an excellent belay.

5) 30 feet. Cross the gully and climb obliquely left up a mossy wall to a junction with Route 1. This is followed to the top.

VARIATION FINISH.

1) 70 feet. From the top of the second pitch climb straight up the arête on large holds, then up easy rocks to the top.

I

ZERO ROUTE.—115 feet. Very Difficult. Quite a pleasant litt climb. Starts about 10 feet to the right of the obvio nail-marked start of Route 1, at a steep little wa Cairn.

(1) 45 feet. The 20-foot wall with a small rock ledge hal way is followed by easier slabs to a flake-belay. Th pitch is usually wet.

(2) 70 feet. A very shallow groove slanting right in th rocks on the left of the belay is followed. The climbin is steep, but holds are good. Near a small overhan; half-way up, the rock requires care. A block-belay reached at a junction with Route 1.

ROUTE 1.—150 feet. Difficult.

(1) 15 feet. A short wall is climbed to a holly-tree belay.

(2) 30 feet. Climb a mossy slab on the left, then step to th right to a rock nose leading to a grass ledge just belov and to the right of, a small overhang. Small belay.

(3) 25 feet. Traverse 8 feet to the right and then climb direc Where the buttress steepens step left to a small ledg in the groove where there is a good belay high up o the extreme left.

(4) 30 feet. Step back to the right and climb direct to rock ledge with small belays.

(5) 50 feet. The easy-angled slabs give good holds to th top.

ROUTE 1·5.—135 feet. Very Difficult. Runs up the fac midway between Routes 1 and 2. The lower portio is dirty and unpleasant in wet conditions.

(1) 40 feet. A very mossy crack is climbed for about 10 feet

A move is then made out to the right followed by an
ascent to a stance and spike-belay on the right.

3) 35 feet. The wall above, the overhang being turned on
the left. Belay. (Top of Pitch 2, Route 2.)

4) 60 feet. Easy climbing up the slabs between Routes 1
and 2.

ROUTE 2.—145 feet. Difficult. Starts from a grass terrace
just to the left of and slightly higher than Route 1.

1) 45 feet. A severe crack in a vertical wall can be turned
on the left. Climb round to the right under a holly
bush to a grass ledge and oak-tree belay.

2) 40 feet. Traverse 10 feet to the right, then up the steep
wall on good holds to a belay in the groove on the
right.

3) 60 feet. Step back to the left and climb the easy-angled
slabs to the finish.

SCOUT'S BELT.—285 feet. Very Difficult. Traverses the crag
from right to left. Though rather artificial and
vegetatious in places it provides quite pleasant climbing. Starts at the foot of Zero Route. (q.v.)

1) 45 feet. The first pitch of Zero Route.

2) 70 feet. From the belay climb the wall to the left of the
open groove on the second pitch of Zero Route,
working leftwards after a few feet, and finishing by
the arête on Route 1.

3) 25 feet. A descending traverse is made to the belay in
the groove on Route 2. (Top of second pitch.)

4) 55 feet. The next belay is the tree visible round the
arête on the left. It is attained by traversing grass

ledges to cross a heathery groove on to the arête whic
is descended to the tree.

(5)   50 feet.   Cross the juniper ledge into a corner level wit
the top of an obvious horizontal crack.   Good hol
enable a short descent to be made down the stee
vegetatious rocks below the corner, when a risir
traverse over bulging rocks, using the horizont
crack as handhold, leads to a large spike belay.

(6)   40 feet.   An easy traverse upwards brings one to th
scree gully.   If desired, the summit of the crag ca
then be attained by various routes on the well-scratche
slabs.

Lower Scout Crag

Situated a few hundred feet directly below the main crag
offers two short, but steep, climbs and abundant opportunit
for abseiling practice.   A pleasant approach to the higher crag

The better of the two climbs, The Slab (Very Difficult
starts from a right-angled corner in the centre of the crag an
runs up the right-hand bounding wall.   The route bear
diagonally right to the arête, then back left into the final crack
The crack contains a movable chockstone which is nevertheles
perfectly sound.   Tree belay.

A few feet to the left of The Slab a cracked wall gives a steep
climb on magnificent holds.   There are several obviou
alternatives, most of them interesting and of 'Very Difficult
standard.   Between Lower Scout Crag and the road the Spli
Boulder provides some amusing problems.   The crack on its
lower side, well seen from the road, is awkward to start and is
technically severe.   By combining routes on the lower crags
with climbs in White Ghyll and on Pavey Ark an enjoyable i

rcuitous approach to the Pikes is obtained, comparable with
ιe more usual one via Middlefell and Gimmer.

ᵗarn Crag, of similar interest to Scout Crag, is suitable for
ᵗaining purposes or as an aperitif to the more serious fare on
avey Ark. Situated on the immediate right of Mill Ghyll,
ɔme 200 feet below the level of Stickle Tarn, it is best reached
y following the right-hand path up the Ghyll until a track
ɛads off right to the foot of the Crag.

A broad buttress, on which the first four routes lie, is
ɛparated from the well-defined ridge containing Route 1 and
Ϊib and Wall by a grassy amphitheatre. A tongue of vegetatious
ɔck, topped by a conspicuous oak, runs up the middle of the
ɪmphitheatre to join the steeper rocks above. Here lies
Ϊlandish. None of the routes is continuously steep and the
ɛnse of exposure is usually slight.

West Buttress.—130 feet. Difficult. Starts at the foot of
ᵗhe first steep wall, marked by a holly-tree high on the left.
1) 40 feet. The wall is climbed, passing just to the right
    of the holly-tree, to a grass ledge below a groove.
    Belay.
2) 10 feet. Up the groove to another grass ledge and belay.
3) 80 feet. Traverse left for 10 feet to the foot of a rib
    which is climbed for 30 feet, when easy rocks lead to
    the summit.

Route 2.—130 feet. Difficult. Starts at the lowest point of
    the buttress, 15 feet to the right of West Buttress.
1) 30 feet. Steep rocks lead to a grassy corner. Belay above.
2) 40 feet. Straight up on good holds to a grass ledge and
    belay.

(3) 60 feet. Broken rocks are followed to the top.

HEATHER SLAB.—135 feet. Very difficult. Starts just to the left of an aspen-tree, at the foot of a smooth, triangular slab.

(1) 30 feet. Straight up the slab and the rather awkward groove at its apex to an exit on the left into an earthy recess. Tiny spike-belay on right.

(2) 45 feet. Traverse 15 feet left and climb a steep but easy corner onto a sloping, grassy ledge. Good spike-belay.

(3) 60 feet. The groove on the right gives onto an easy arête. This is followed until broken rocks lead rightward to the summit.

ORCHID.—285 feet. Severe in boots. Necessarily artificial but of some technical interest. Starts 5 feet to the right of the aspen-tree below a steep crack.

(1) 50 feet. The crack, grassy at first, is entered from the right via a smooth slab. Its steeper continuation then leads up to a grass ledge.

(2) 70 feet. Up the shallow chimney ahead, passing a small pinnacle. Finish by climbing out to the left and so up to a ledge.

(3) 50 feet. Traverse right, passing a rowan-tree in a corner, and continuing to the left end of a bilberry ledge. From here a short ascent leads to the foot of a groove in a corner. Flake-belay on right.

(4) 35 feet. The groove is a little awkward at the top. Above it step right and in a few feet reach a grass ledge below a slab. Spike-belay low down.

5) 80 feet. The left-hand edge of the slab and broken rocks lead to the top.

BLANDISH.—180 feet. Very difficult. Starts from a prominent oak situated high up the tongue of vegetatious rock which runs up the middle of the amphitheatre. The tree is gained by an easy scramble.

1) 20 feet. The wall behind the tree is climbed to a bilberry ledge.

2) 70 feet. The steep rib above is climbed, using a thin crack on its left, until a traverse to the right leads to a heather corner.

3) 40 feet. A short wall is ascended to a ledge.

4) 50 feet. A steep groove in the wall ahead is followed by easier rocks leading to the top.

RIB AND WALL.—130 feet. Difficult. To the right of the grassy amphitheatre is the prominent ridge of Route 1. 10 feet to the left of this a subsidiary rib runs up to abut against its left-hand wall. Starts at the foot of the rib.

1) 75 feet. Straight up the middle of the rib to a ledge. Belay 20 feet higher on the wall.

2) 55 feet. Continue up to a small ledge, then slightly left to finish up a short, steep groove.

ROUTE 1.—105 feet. Difficult. The well-marked route up the right-hand ridge of the Crag. Starts rather to the left of the foot of the ridge.

1) 45 feet. A short ascent and a traverse to the nose are followed by straightforward climbing up to a good stance and belay.

(2)   60 feet.   Broken rocks to the finish.

HARRISON STICKLE.   The summit crags of Harrison Stickle
impressive as they are when seen from a distance, prov
disappointingly broken on close inspection.   Several route
have, however, been recorded on the west face but none seem
to merit description except those given below.   Innumerable
variations are possible.

HARRISTICKORNER.—85 feet.   Very difficult.   Lies up the
   corner where the north and west faces meet.   Steep
   with good holds.   Starts at the foot of a well-scratched
   corner.
(1)   15 feet.   Up the corner to a ledge and belay on the left.
(2)   30 feet.   After one step to the right climb the wall above
   to a small stance and belay.
(3)   40 feet.   Traverse 10 feet horizontally to the right,
   then upwards and slightly left via a somewhat mossy
   groove to the top.

PORPHYRY SLAB.—240 feet.   Very difficult.   Starts in a grassy
   bay 200 feet to the right of Harristickorner, below a
   broad, mossy slab.
(1)   100 feet.   The easy heathery ribs on the right lead to a
   triangular grass ledge at the foot of a crack.
(2)   30 feet.   The wall on the left with a move out to a bracket
   belay.
(3)   30 feet.   The pleasant slab is climbed more or less direct,
   moving left at the top to a ledge and belay.
(4)   40 feet.   From right-hand end of ledge climb diagonally
   right to a good ledge.
(5)   30 feet.   The wall on the right leads easily to a belay at
   the foot of the final obstacle.

6) 10 feet. The short wall is overcome with some difficulty.

WALLER'S CRACK is a stiff 40-foot problem round to the left from Harristickorner. It is reached by means of a short, grassy scramble.

SIDE PIKE is situated on the extreme right of Lingmoor Fell as viewed from the new Dungeon Ghyll Hotel. The climbs lie on the steep east end in the gap between the Pike and the Fell.

SPIDER CRACK.—110 feet. Severe. The prominent crack, overhanging near the bottom, a few yards to the left of the stone wall. It can prove quite awkward in wet weather due to the sloping nature of the handholds.
(1) 25 feet. The overhang is avoided by climbing the steep wall on the left for about 15 feet followed by a rather awkward traverse right into a niche in the crack. Belay.
(2) 35 feet. The crack is climbed direct, on good holds for the first 20 feet, followed by a more delicate section. A large heather shelf is reached, with a belay a few feet higher.
(3) 50 feet. Finish up mossy rocks to the left or steep grass to the right. The former is probably preferable.

LIMPET GROOVES.—80 feet. Very severe. The obvious grooves on the immediate right of the large detached pinnacle at the foot of the crag near its left-hand end. Though short, the route has considerable interest and difficulty. Ascend the right wall of the bottom groove for about 10 feet when a long stride can be made into the groove. Chockstone for running belay. From a standing position above the chockstone a traverse is then made across the vertical right wall on good holds to a small ledge. The overhanging groove above is then climbed direct by means of a series of semi-layback moves, and is strenuous. A belay will be found about 10 feet left of the finish.

TOWER CLIMB. Moderate. The following description is taken from the *Journal of the Fell & Rock Climbing Club* :—

The climb is a conspicuous arête high up on the south side of Side Pike overlooking Blea Tarn.

(1) 30 feet. A wall. Then traverse 15 feet left.

(2) 20 feet. A groove.

(3) 40 feet. An arête followed by a 10-foot slab. Ascend grass slope for about 40 feet to jammed blocks which are climbed by a 10-foot chimney on the left. The summit of Side Pike is within 100 feet over easy ground.

RAVEN CRAG, WALTHWAITE

RAVEN CRAG, WALTHWAITE, is a conspicuous outcrop lying just behind the farm and very near to the road from Chapel Stile to Red Bank. It offers the following climbs, described from left to right.

ROUTE 1.   90 feet. Severe. Starts above the holly-tree at the extreme left of the crag. The easiest recognised route on the crag, it is well-marked, commencing with a slight traverse to the left followed by an ascent to the right.

ROUTE 2. 80 feet. Severe. Steep and interesting. Starts at a small ash-tree at the lowest point of the crag and rises over a small nose to an oak-tree 60 feet up. 10 feet left of this tree the route follows a short scoop, traverses right for 5 feet, then inclines left again until, at an overhanging rib, a chimney leads off to the right to the finish.

DEUTERUS.—120 feet. Very severe. An exposed route. The rock requires care in places, particularly on the long traverse in the second pitch. Starts a few feet to the right of Route 2.

(1) 30 feet. Ascend the wall direct to a good ledge and holly-tree belay.

(2) 90 feet. Ascend the overhanging scoop on the right, the first few feet being the hardest. Move left and up to a grassy recess on Route 2. (Spike on right for running belay.) Traverse to the right round the rib and across the wall to a junction with Protus at a recess and doubtful spike. Finish up Protus.

PROTUS.—90 feet. Very severe. Steep and exposed, with considerable technical difficulty. Starts at a holly-tree about 30 feet to the right of Deuterus. There is an oak-tree on the left and an elm-tree above on the right.

(1) 30 feet. From the holly-tree work upwards to the right, surmounting an awkward bulge. Belay round elm-tree.

(2) 60 feet. Descend a few feet and traverse delicately left and up a few feet, crossing a rib into a groove by means of an awkward movement. Step round to the left and pull out of the groove onto the exposed wall on the left, passing a triangular overhang. Ascend the wall

to a recess containing a doubtful spike. A short traverse to the right is followed by a direct ascent to the top on good holds.

OAK HOWE NEEDLE.—This rock lies fairly high on the south-west ridge of Lingmoor, half-an-hour from the New Hotel. It is best approached from there by crossing the bridge almost opposite, passing through the farm-yard, then turning left and keeping fairly low until the ridge itself is reached. The abrupt ascent of this is simpler than crossing through the heavy juniper higher up the fellside. The climbs are short and few, and as such, unworthy of a special visit.

The Needle is split from east to west, the fissure thus formed giving a severe crack on either side. Both lead to the same crevasse, the east in 35 feet, the west in 25 feet, with the last bit overhanging. From here a 10-foot chimney reaches the top.

An easy way on the south side reaches the foot of this same chimney in 15 feet.

The shoulder on the north side can be reached either by a dirty groove in the north-west slabs, or by the steeper and cleaner North-east Wall.

From this shoulder, a severe slab to the left of the west crack leads to the same final 10-foot pitch.

KETTLE CRAG.—This is the lowest crag on the slopes of Pike o' Blisco, facing Wall End Farm. There are four short climbs rising to the left out of a wide grassy gully. The first, an arête, starts 60 feet above the gully's foot. The Major Slab starts between two ash-trees 50 feet higher up the gully. A few feet higher the Minor Slab leads leftwards via a detached block and a variaiton route exists just to the right of this.

GLADSTONE KNOTT.—Situated 400 yards from the head of Crinkle Gill, on the left, and facing east. It has five climbable chimneys. The rock is poor with overmuch vegetation and the crag cannot be recommended. The following descriptions are by J. R. Tyson :—

First Chimney.—Difficult. Climb up the left wall (rotten rock) to the first chockstone, then use both walls past the second chockstone to a good stance, a distance of 35 feet in all. Next climb the rib forming the left wall and bridge and proceed up slabs on the right to a stance with a good belay (20 feet). Next use both sides of the chimney for 15 feet to a good stance. For the next 12 feet use the chockstone at the top by holding either side ; this is difficult but can be avoided on the right. The next 15 feet consist of broken rocks and vegetation. To finish, climb the rib in the centre, or the scoop on either side.

Second Chimney.—First moderate climbing, much vegetation, for 25 feet. Similar climbing for 30 feet but rather more difficult. Climb now to the right of the rib, and use the edge, then over the rib to a good stance under the chockstone. For the next 30 feet traverse the left wall and up a rib (30 feet) to the top.

Third Chimney.—Not a climb, a garden.

Fourth Chimney.—Very deep, black, and conspicuous. Climb 25 feet up the right wall and chockstones to a cave. The next 30 feet of climbing is either up the left wall, or bridging, with a window-pitch finish. The final 35 feet consist of a moderate chockstone, some pasture, and a short pitch with a scrambling finish.

Fifth Chimney.—Lies 15 yards to the right of the Fourth. Starts with 20 feet of easy rock and grass to the foot of the chimney. Moderate climbing of 30 feet to a cave. (A variation start goes up a rock trough leading to the cave ; this is moderate, but cuts out the grass and loose rock at the start.) After this come 15 feet of back-and-knee work ; rock very wet and rotten.

EASEDALE

Holly-tree Crack.—120 feet. Very difficult. This climb lies up the obvious crag 100 yards behind the quarry on the Helm Crag track from Easedale. It starts in a triangular nook and is served by a large tree as cairn.

(1) 40 feet. Climb up a steep crack via a useful tree to a block balcony.

(2) 30 feet. Move a few feet to the right, then straight ahead over questionable blocks to a holly tree. This can be used as a belay ; one must climb through it.

(3) 30 feet. Continue up a grassy gully to the plantation above.

(4) 20 feet. Move 10 feet to the right along the grass ledge and finish up the short wall above.

Gibson Knott.—This steep, vegetation-covered crag lies on the north slopes of Far Easedale, a little above the stepping stones and some 400 feet above the valley. It has two wet-weather climbs of only moderate interest.

ROUTE 1.—235 feet, only 40 feet of climbing. Difficult.

1) 40 feet. Towards the right-hand end of the crag a subsidiary buttress juts out. Easy scrambling up this (avoidable on the left) leads to a terrace.

2) 40 feet. Climb slightly right up the steep wall above, and at a distance of 30 feet step left into a very short chimney leading to another terrace.

3) 130 feet. Easy scrambling midst the junipers leads to the top of the crag.

ROUTE 2.—210 feet. Difficult. Near the left-hand corner is a steep chimney, 40 feet high, marked by a large triangle of juniper bushes at its foot.

(1) 25 feet of grass form the left-hand side of this triangle to the foot of the chimney.

(2) 15 feet. Climb the scooped wall on the left to a comfortable ledge and belays.

(3) 30 feet. A 20-foot mossy wall above leads via a steep turf finish to a terrace running leftwards to belaying blocks.

(4) 45 feet. Start left of these blocks, and after only a few feet a very difficult upward traverse round a corner to the right enters a 6-foot chimney which is climbed. Belay 20 feet higher on the grass terrace.

An alternative pitch leads rather higher at the start, then by an easier traverse to the right to the top of the same 6-foot chimney.

(5) 120 feet. An easy zigzag route leads first 40 feet leftwards then rightwards to the top of the crag.

BLEA RIGG CLIMB.—185 feet. Very difficult. This crag lies above Easedale Tarn, on the route to Pavey Ark and some twenty minutes' walk from the Tarn. The rock is very steep and somewhat broken, but as yet has only one climb. This lies to the leftmost end, starting above a broken tree at the immediate left edge of a huge fan of vegetation which splits the crag centrally.

(1) 70 feet. Easy scrambling upwards to the right via a grassy ledge leads to a corner with a large jammed boulder on the left.

(2) 25 feet. Up and over this boulder to a grass terrace with large block belay.

(3) 30 feet. Traverse the wall to the arête on the right and climb on small holds to the right of the ridge until a good flat ledge is reached ; unfortunately offering no satisfactory belay.

(4) 10 feet. The grassy corner above leads to a cave with an A.1 belay.

(5) 50 feet. The open chimney above is difficult for 10 feet, climbed either in the chimney or on the right, but then becomes an easy grassy gully leading to the finishing balcony.

DEER BIELD CRAG is a small, but impressively steep, crag situated on the left-hand side of Far Easedale, some three hundred feet above the path and about an hour's easy walk from Grasmere. It may be reached from Great Langdale (New Hotel) in a slightly longer time by way of Mill Ghyll and Stickle and Codale Tarns ; or Raw Head (F. & R.C.C. Hut) by striking up the fell side and crossing Easedale just above the Tarn, when a further short ascent leads over the next spur to the top of the Crag.

The most prominent feature of the Crag is its central buttress, actually completely detached. Two outstanding

limbs make use of the fissure between this buttress and the
parent crag—the Crack on the left and the Chimney on the
right; the buttress itself remains unclimbed despite many
attempts on this particular 'last great problem.' To the right
of the Chimney a short outcrop gives rise to the only other
route so far discovered on this fine crag.

DEER BIELD CRACK.—170 feet. Very severe. A climb of
>   great character and interest, requiring considerable
>   energy and perseverance. The famous chimney pitch
>   is probably unique of its type, and the final overhang
>   is sufficiently problematical to leave the outcome in
>   doubt until the very end. May often be found
>   reasonably dry after, or even during, a period of rain.
>   Starts at an upstanding flake-belay slightly to the left
>   of the lowest point of the buttress.

1)   20 feet. The crack immediately above the belay is
>   climbed for about 6 feet, when a long stride is made to a
>   nook on the right. A few feet higher is a stance and
>   pedestal-belay.

2)   15 feet. Climb the slab on the left for 10 feet and pull
>   round on good holds into the crack. This is followed
>   to the first Raven's Nest. Awkward thread-belay.

3)   25 feet. The chimney on the left. A comfortable ledge
>   with a small tree and large block-belay is reached.

4)   20 feet. The shallow chimney above requires a little
>   care in the handling of some large blocks high on the
>   right. The second Nest is gained, and a remarkable
>   view of the Chimney—but insufficient room for a
>   through route.

5)   35 feet. This is the crucial pitch. The crack now attains
>   the proportions of a chimney, very narrow at first,

wide in its middle section, then finally narrow agai
with an overhang jutting out above. It is best climbe
deeply inside as long as possible with one's back o
the vertical left wall and feet on the slightly impendin
right wall. Traverse out under the overhang an
ascend the last few strenuous feet to a small ledge o
the left with a fine chockstone belay 6 feet above.

(6) 40 feet. The crack now narrows, permitting wedgin
tactics. It eases after 10 feet and leads to a large reces
below a super Amen Corner.

(7) 15 feet. The crack in the right-hand corner above over
hangs considerably in both directions. A 12-inc
wide wall some distance to the left will be found usefu
until splendid holds allow a pull-over to be made o
to the top of the crag.

DEER BIELD CHIMNEY.—200 feet. Severe. An outstandin
climb of its kind, suitable for most weather conditions
The delicately poised blocks above pitch 4 should b
treated with great respect. The start is obvious
about 12 paces to the right of Deer Bield Crack.

(1) 25 feet. Scramble up a grass ledge to the foot of th
chimney proper.

(2) 45 feet. The chimney is climbed for 15 feet, when a
rather awkward 10-foot scoop leads out to the right.
Traverse back into the chimney bed.

(3) 15 feet. The jammed boulders above are reached by
bridging.

(4) 25 feet. A way is threaded upwards through further
jammed stones to a large and comfortable recess with
a view into Deer Bield Crack.

(5) 15 feet. Climb out on the right to reach a stance below

the overhanging blocks. High flake-belay, and a tree-belay at one's feet.

) 25 feet. A delicate traverse out onto the right wall followed by a short, awkward ascent lands one above the blocks. A few feet higher is a comfortable Sentry Box.

') 15 feet. Ascend the chimney above to an airy view-point.

) 20 feet. The smooth crack leads to a large, sloping platform. It is possible to walk off the climb here. (The original route avoided pitches 7 and 8 by following the grassy gully which runs up to the right from the Sentry Box. After 20 feet a short crack is climbed until one can step back left to the same sloping platform.)

) 15 feet. A strenuous oblique hand-traverse leads upwards to the right to the top of the buttress.

MONKEY PUZZLE.—150 feet. Severe. An amusing climb with unexpected situations on the small pear-shaped buttress to the right of the Chimney. Starts at a corner formed by the overhanging foot of the buttress and a sharp little arête on its left.

) 50 feet. The steep slab in the corner leads, with an awkward move, into the easy-looking groove above. This groove, grassy in its upper portion, is ascended to a spike-belay on the right wall.

) 25 feet. The pleasant slab above the belay. A large block-belay is reached on the ' roof.'

) 60 feet. Traverse right to a tree on the edge of the buttress. The tree is useful as a take-off for the ascent of the arête above which leads to the top.

SOUTH-EAST FACE—GIMMER CRAG

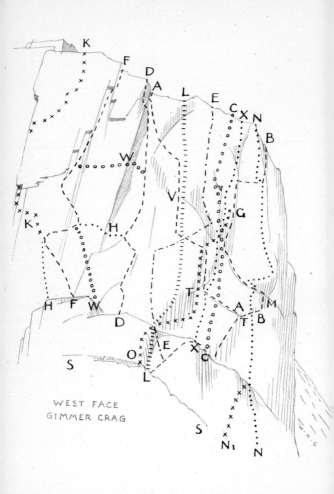

WEST FACE
GIMMER CRAG

WEST FACE—GIMMER CRAG

NORTH-WEST FACE—GIMMER CRAG

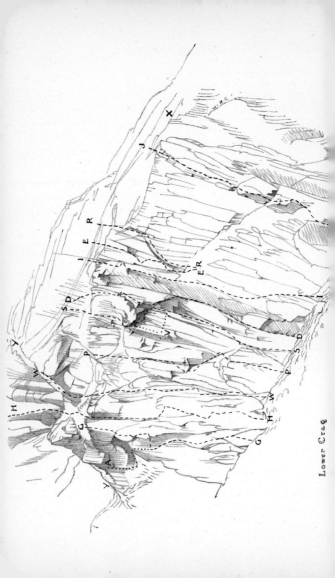

Lower Crag

WHITE GHYLL
LOWER CRAG

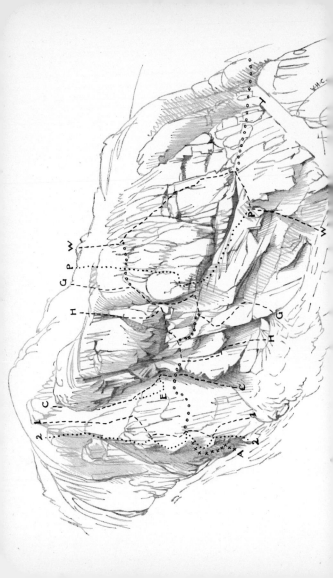

WHITE GHYLL
UPPER CRAG

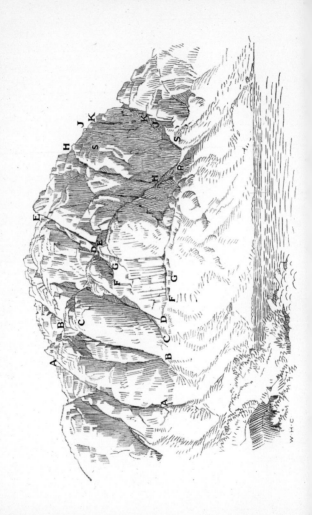

PAVEY ARK

RAVEN CRAG
GREAT LANGDALE

K

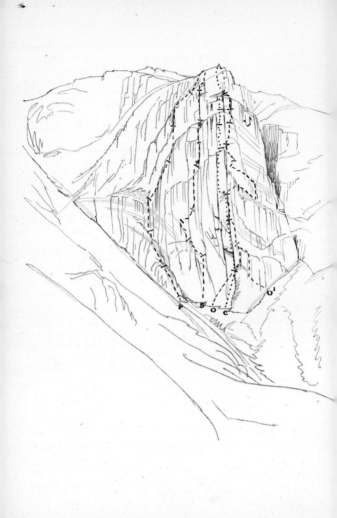

BOWFELL BUTTRESS

CLASSIFIED LIST OF CLIMBS

LIST OF FIRST ASCENTS

	Jack's Rake. Date indefinite (between 1870–80)	R. Pendlebury.
82	Great Gully, Pavey Ark	W. P. Haskett-Smith.
82	North Gully, Bowfell Buttress	W. P. Haskett-Smith.
82	North-west Gully, Gimmer Crag	W. P. Haskett-Smith.
86	June. Little Gully, Pavey Ark	W. P. Haskett-Smith.
92	April. Gwynne's Chimney	H. A. Gwynne and party.

W. P. Haskett-Smith had previously descended the Chimney. 18 Mar. 1923. Variation. R. S. T. Chorley, H. P. Cain, W. G. Pape.

97	April 20. Bowfell Links, No. 4	C. R. B. Storry. G. H. McKilburn. J. W. Davies.
97	Sept. Bowfell Links, Nos. 5 and 6	C. R. B. Storry. G. D. Abraham. A. P. Abraham. G. H. McKilburn.
98	Oct. 1. Rake End Chimney	C. W. Barton.

1902 May 24. Bowfell Buttress   T. Shaw.

                                                                              G. H. Craig.

                                                                               G. R. West.

                                                                               C. Hargreaves.

                                                                              L. J. Oppenheimer.

30 Sept. 1916. Alternative start. H. M. Kelly.

20 Sept. 1919. Variation by Chimney. T. H. Somervell, Somervell.

1902 Nov. 2. Gimmer Chimney   E. Rigby.

                                                                               J. Sandison.

                                                                               A. S. Thomson.

The more direct and severe chimney, 6th pitch (see Bracket a͟ Slab Climb), was climbed as an alternative by H. M. Kelly a͟ J. B. Meldrum, 18 May 1918.

1902 Nov. 2.   South-east Lower   E. Rigby.
              Traverse, Gimmer Crag

1903 April 7. 'A' Route, Gimmer   E. Rigby.
              Crag   D. Leighton.

                                                                               J. Sandison.

1907 April.   Crescent Climb   F. Botterill.

                                                                               W. E. Palmer.

N.B.—The Gully portion of this climb was done by C. W. Barto͟ 24 October 1899.

10 May 1913. Variation on Slabs. S. W. Herford, C. W. Marsha͟

6 Aug. 1909. Variation of Start. S. H. Gordon, H. S. Lieschin͟

1907 May 26. Oliverson's Varia-   C. H. Oliverson.
              tion, Gimmer Crag   G. C. Turner.

                                                                               F. B. Kershaw.

1907	May 26. Lyon's Crawl, Gimmer Crag.	H. B. Lyon. J. Stables. A. S. Thomson.
1907	July 7. ' B ' Route, Gimmer Crag	H. B. Lyon. J. Stables. A. S. Thomson.
1907	Sept. 22. Junipall (Raven) Gully, Gimmer Crag	Fell and Rock Party. Names not recorded.
1908	Oct. Blea Rigg, Easedale	G. C. Turner. J. Stables.
1908	Oct. Deer Bield (Right Chimney)	J. Stables. G. C. Turner.
1909	Aug. 15. Pike O'Stickle Gully	W. B. Brunskill.
1910	Mar. 22. Gibson's Chimney, Pavey Ark	H. Bishop. C. D. Yeomans.
1910	Mar. 27. Elephant's Nose Buttress, Pavey Ark	J. A. Stoop. C. D. Yeomans.
1910	Mar. 28. Bennison's Chimney, Pavey Ark	W. E. Bennison. A. E. Burns. T. H. Seaton. C. D. Yeomans.

1910	Oct. 22.	Beehive Buttress (beyond White Ghyll)	C. H. Oliverson. Mrs. C. H. Oliverson.
1910	Oct. 24.	Holly-tree Climb (Beehive)	C. H. Oliverson. G. J. Boden. Mrs. C. H. Oliverson.
1910	Dec. 4.	Beehive Buttress (South Route)	C. H. Oliverson. G. E. T. Thorpe. Mrs. C. H. Oliverson.
1911	Sept. 24.	Middle Fell Buttress	J. Laycock. S. W. Herford. A. R. Thomson.
1913	May 13.	Gladstone Knott First Chimney	H. Bishop. C. D. Yeomans.
1916	Oct. 2.	Gladstone Knott Fourth Chimney	H. M. Kelly.
1918	Aug. 3.	' C ' Route, Gimmer Crag	A. P. Wilson. G. H. Jackson. A. Brundritt.
1919	May 31.	' D ' Route, Gimmer Crag	G. S. Bower. P. R. Masson.
1920	April 18.	Stony Buttress, Pavey Ark	G. S. Bower. A. W. Wakefield.

1920   June 19. Crescent Slabs,   G. S. Bower.
            Pavey Ark   A. W. Wakefield.

1920   June 20. Ash-tree Slabs,   G. S. Bower.
            Gimmer Crag   A. W. Wakefield.

1921   Jan. 30. Harristickorner   G. S. Bower.
                J. C. Appleyard.

1921   Mar. 20. Main Wall Traverse   G. S. Bower.
                F. Graham.

Variations :—5 June 1921. A. and G. Ackerley. 1931, W. Heaton
Cooper, W. Eden-Smith, Miss U. Heaton Cooper. 21 Apr. 1935.
W. S. Farrar, C. G. Wickham.

1921   July 28. Tarn Crag Buttress,   J. A. Garrick.
            Mill Ghyll   W. L. Tulip.

1922   June 8. Juniper Buttress,   C. F. Holland.
            Gimmer Crag   A. S. Piggott.
                Morley Wood.

1922   Sept. 6. Cambridge Climb   W. T. Elmslie.
            (Bowfell)   A. de St. C. Walsh.

1922   Oct. Scout Crag (Rts. 1 & 2)   F. Graham.

1923   April 19. Gladstone Knott   W. T. Elmslie.
            Second Chimney   A. de St. Walsh.

| 1923 | Aug. 8. Bracket and Slab Climb, Gimmer Crag | H. B. Lyon. J. Herbert. |

12 Aug. 1923. First Ascent including Chimney. H. B. Lyon, J. Herbert, Miss M. M. Barker, H. P. Cain, J. B. Wilton.

| 1923 | Aug. 10. White Ghyll Chimney | H. B. Lyon. J. Herbert. H. P. Cain. |

10 April 1948. Variation to Pitch 3. J. D. Teare.

| 1923 | Sept. 3. Chimney Buttress, Gimmer Crag | H. B. Lyon. G. Ackerley. J. Herbert. |

| 1924 | Aug. 11. ' E ' Route, Gimmer Crag | J. A. Wray. G. Basterfield. |

| 1924 | Aug. 11. Right-hand Wall, Bowfell | M. de Selincourt. Miss B. Ritchie. |

| 1924 | Sept. 1. The Neckband | M. de Selincourt. |

| 1924 | Sept. 7. Holly-tree Crack (Easedale) | M. de Selincourt. |

| 1924 | Crescent Wall, Pavey Ark | M. de Selincourt. |

| 1925 | Mar. 18. Herdwick Buttress, Gimmer Crag | F. Graham. |

| 1925 | April. Gibson Knott (Easedale) 1 and 2 | A. R. Thomson. A. Dibona. |

926 May 13. Pallid Slabs,   G. S. Bower.
      Gimmer Crag   A. W. Wakefield.
                             H. V. Hughes.

926 June 27. Diphthong,   Morley Wood.
      Gimmer Crag   G. S. Bower.
                             A. B. Reynolds.
                             F. Frischmann.

       22 July 1934. Direct Finish. J. R. Files, J. E. B. Wright.

926 Aug. 14. Gladstone's Finger   W. T. Elmslie.
      (Gladstone Knott)   D. Duncan.
                             T. Baird.

927 July 10. Hiatus, Gimmer   G. S. Bower.
      Crag   A. B. Reynolds.
                             A. W. Wakefield.
                             G. G. Macphee.

       First climbed on a rope from above by G. Basterfield and J. R.
       Tyson in 1926.
       1931. Variation Finish. A. W. Bridge, A. B. Hargreaves.
       21 Sept. 1936. Grooves Traverse. R. V. M. Barry, E. G. Harper.
       28 Aug. 1949. Grooves Superdirect. A. R. Dolphin, J. Bloor.

1927 Aug. 17. Black Warrs,   W. T. Elmslie and
      Pike o' Blisco   others.

1928 May 5. The Crack, Gimmer   A. B. Reynolds.
      Crag   G. G. Macphee.

       4 April 1928. First ascended with a rope from above by A. B.
       Reynolds and H. G. Knight.

1928 May 6. Borstal Buttress,   A. B. Reynolds.
      Bowfell   G. G. Macphee.
                             R. C. Abbatt.

1928	May 13. Asterisk, Gimmer Crag	H. S. Gross. G. Basterfield. B. Tyson.
1928	Joas, Gimmer Crag	G. G. Macphee. A. B. Reynolds.
1929	Aug. 8. Musgrave's Traverse, Gimmer Crag	J. A. Musgrave. Miss N. Ridyard.
1930	Feb. 16. Deer Bield Crack, Far Easedale	A. T. Hargreaves. G. G. Macphee.
1930	Aug. 10. Raven Crag Buttress, Great Langdale	S. Watson. D. Usher. R. Holmes. W. Cowen. N. Middleton.
1930	Sept. 15. Route 1, White Ghyll Slabs	G. Barker. A. T. Hargreaves.
1931	April 30. Plaque Route, Bowfell	H. M. Kelly. Blanche Eden-Smith.
1931	May 20. Central Route, Bowfell	H. M. Kelly. Blanche Eden-Smith
1932	Sept. 24. Sinister Slabs, Bowfell	A. T. Hargreaves. G. G. Macphee.
1933	June 28. Stoats' Crack, Pavey Ark	B. R. Record. J. R. Jenkins.

9 Aug. 1945. Variation to pitch 7. H. A. Carsten, E. H. Phillips.

1933 July 21. Kettle Crag Climbs,   J. Wharton.
         Pike o' Blisco   F. G. Stangle.

1933   Route 2, White Ghyll Slabs   S. Cross.
                                    E. Fallowfield.
                                    C. Tatham.
       21 Aug. 1947. Alternative Start. A. Gregory, J. W. Tucker

1936   Sept. 21. Barry's Traverse,   R. V. M. Barry.
            Gimmer Crag   E. G. Harper.

1938   April 17. Hyphen, Gimmer   A. Mullan.
            Crag   G. Parkinson.

1939   April 16. Zero, Scout Crag   S. Thompson.
                                    J. Diamond.

1939   May 6. Deception, Pavey   S. H. Cross.
            Ark   Alice M. Nelson.

1939   Aug. 26. Wailing Wall,   S. H. Cross.
            Pavey Ark   A. T. Hargreaves.
                                    Ruth Hargreaves.
                                    Alice Nelson.

1940   Crow's Nest Direct, Gimmer   S. Thompson.
            Crag   Phyllis White
                                    A. Mullan.
                                    Valerie Bolton.
                                    J. Ashton.
       13 Jan. 1946. Alternative Start. A. R. Dolphin, A. B. Gilchrist.

L

1940	April 18. Prelude, Gimmer Crag	A. H. Griffin. L. K. Griffin. J. Diamond.
1940	Sept. 15. North-west Arête, Gimmer Crag	R. J. Birkett. V. Veevers.
1940	Sept. 15. The Gordian Knot, White Ghyll	J. W. Haggas. Miss E. Bull.
1940	Sept. 29. Interlude, Gimmer Crag	J. Ashton. J. Diamond. J. Brady.
1940	Oct. 13. Wall End, Gimmer Crag	J. Ashton. J. Diamond. J. Apted. Lyna Kellett.
1940	Oct. 13. Paleface, Gimmer Crag	J. Ashton. J. Apted. Lyna Kellett. J. Diamond.
1941	May 4. ' F ' Route, Gimmer Crag	R. J. Birkett. V. Veevers.
1941	June 27. Bilberry Buttress, Raven Crag	C. F. Rolland. J. F. Renwick.
1941	Aug. 3. Bachelor Crack, Gimmer Crag	R. J. Birkett. V. Veevers. J. Craven.

1942.	May 1. Right-hand Wall Traverse, Bowfell	G. B. Elliott. H. M. Elliott.
1942	May. Bowfell Buttress Girdle	S. H. Cross. A. T. Hargreaves. Ruth Hargreaves. Alice Cross.
1942	June 17. Bracken Route, Pavey Ark	G. B. Elliott. A. Mullan. S. A. Williams.
1942	Aug. 11. Porphyry Slab, Harrison Stickle	J. R. Jenkins. J. A. Martinez. M. S. Taylor.
1943	Side Pike Tower	A. F. Airey.
1943	March 14. Cook's Tour, Pavey Ark	J. Cook. G. B. Elliott.

N.B.—The last two pitches were climbed as an extension to Gwynne's Chimney by G. B. Elliott and T. Nicholson in Sept. 1942.

1943	Sept. 5. Savernake, Raven Crag	J. E. Q. Barford. M. P. Ward.
1945	Feb. 26. Peascod's Route, Raven Crag	W. Peascod. J. Pugh.
1945	May 5. Ledge and Groove, Bowfell	R. D. Stevens. G. Stoneley.

L1

| 1945 | Aug. 1. Hollin Groove, White Ghyll | R. J. Birkett. L. Muscroft. |

1945 Aug. 1. Hollin Groove,   R. J. Birkett.
                White Ghyll   L. Muscroft.

1945 Aug. 9. Rake End Wall,   H. A. Carsten.
                Pavey Ark.   E. H. Phillips.

1945 Sept. 24. Nocturne, Gimmer   A. R. Dolphin.
                Crag   J. W. Cook.
      14 April 1946. Groove variation start. D. D. Davies, B. Black
      22 April 1946. Direct start. A. R. Dolphin, D. D. Davies
      D. C. Birch.

1946 Jan. 15. Monkey Puzzle,   A. R. Dolphin.
                Deer Bield Crag   A. B. Gilchrist.

1946 May 5. Ashen Traverse,   D. D. Davies.
                Gimmer Crag   J. M. Hirst.

1946. May 9. White Ghyll Wall   R. J. Birkett.
                                       L. Muscroft.
                                       T. Hill.

1946 June 23. White Ghyll   R. J. Birkett.
                Traverse   L. Muscroft.
                                       T. Hill.

1946 July 31. Spider Crack, Side   R. Bumstead.
                Pike   D. J. Hewitt.
                                       R. L. Plackett.

1947 May 25. Slip Knot, White   R. J. Birkett.
                Ghyll   L. Muscroft.
      20 Sept. 1947. Variation. J. W. Cook, J. W. Haines, J. G. Ball

1947	May 25. Limpet Grooves, Side Pike	A. R. Dolphin. M. Dwyer.
1947	May 26. Garden Path, White Ghyll	A. R. Dolphin. M. Dwyer.
1947.	May 27. Whit's End, Gimmer Crag	A. R. Dolphin. M. Dwyer.
1947	June 23. Protus, Raven Crag Walthwaite	D. C. Birch. A. R. Dolphin.
1947	June 23. Deuterus, Raven Crag Walthwaite	A. R. Dolphin. D. C. Birch. J. W. Cook.
1947	July 12. Oak-tree Wall, Raven Crag	A. Gregory. J. Woods.
1947	July 12. Cartwheel, Gimmer Crag.	J. A. Mullan. A. C. Cain. J. Lancaster.
1947	July 20. Junction Arête, White Ghyll	L. Muscroft. R. J. Birkett.
1947	Aug. 10. Heather Groove, White Ghyll	R. J. Birkett. L. Muscroft. J. Craven.
1947	Aug. 31. Hobson's Choice, Pavey Ark	J. W. Cook. A. R. Dolphin.

Alternate leads.

1947	Sept. 4. Scout's Belt	J. Lancaster. E. Kelly. A. C. Cain.
1947	Oct. 4. Route I·5, Scout Crag	R. A. Ewin. J. R. Files.
1947	Oct. 6. Evening Wall, Raven Crag	A. Gregory. J. W. Tucker. J. Woods.
1948	March 13. Raven Girdle	A. Gregory. J. Ward. J. W. Tucker.
1948	March 29. Revelation, Raven Crag	A. Gregory. B. Black. J. Woods.
1948	April 23. Introduction, Gimmer Crag	D. J. Cameron. A. B. Durrant.
1948	May 9. Haste Not, White Ghyll	R. J. Birkett. L. Muscroft.
1948	Porkers' Parade, White Ghyll	R. J. Birkett. L. Muscroft.
1948	May 15. Samaritan Corner, Gimmer Crag	A. R. Dolphin. J. B. Lockwood. J. Bloor.

1948	May 16. Alph, Pavey Ark	A. R. Dolphin. J. B. Lockwood. J. Bloor.
1948	May 17. Kipling Groove, Gimmer Crag	A. R. Dolphin. J. B. Lockwood.
1948	May 23. Granny Knot, White Ghyll	R. J. Birkett. L. Muscroft.
1948.	May 29. Bluebell Gully, Raven Crag	A. Gregory. J. W. Tucker. J. Ward. C. Peckett.
1948	July 10. Centipede, Raven Crag	A. Gregory. C. Peckett.
1948	Sept. 4. Rambler's Hang- over, Scout Crag	W. Kelsie. D. McKelvie.
1948	Sept. 18. Bluebell Arête, Raven Crag	A. Gregory. J. Renwick.
1948	Oct. 20. Pianissimo, Raven Crag	W. Kelsie. D. McKelvie.
1948	Dec. 12. Route 2, Tarn Crag	A. Gregory. J. Renwick.
1949	Feb. 6. Why Not, White Ghyll	L. Muscroft. R. J. Birkett.

Alternate leads.

| 1949 | April 24. Watson Wall, Raven Crag | A. R. Dolphin. J. Bloor. |

1949　April 24.　Watson Wall,　　A. R. Dolphin.
　　　　　　　Raven Crag　　　　J. Bloor.

1949　April 24.　Baskerville,　　A. R. Dolphin.
　　　　　　　Raven Crag　　　　J. Bloor.

1949　May 2.　Lichen Groove,　　A. C. Cain.
　　　　　　　Gimmer Crag　　　J. Lancaster.

N.B.—A route closely corresponding to the above was climbed solo by J. M. Edwards some ten years before, but could not be identified exactly.

1949　May 15.　Perhaps Not,　　R. J. Birkett.
　　　　　　　White Ghyll　　　L. Muscroft.
　　　　　　　　　Alternate leads.

1949　June 4.　Grey Corner,　　R. D. Stevens.
　　　　　　　Bowfell　　　　　Mrs. J. Stevens.

1949　June 5.　Grey Rib, Bowfell　R. D. Stevens.
　　　　　　　　　　　　　　　Mrs. J. Stevens.

1949　June 7.　Kneewrecker　　A. R. Dolphin.
　　　　　　　Chimney, Raven Crag　J. Bloor.

1949　June 19.　Do Not, White　　R. J. Birkett.
　　　　　　　Ghyll　　　　　　L. Muscroft.

This was the second pitch only, climbed as an alternative finish to Slip Knot. The independent start was added by K. Heaton and A. Heaton on Oct. 9, 1949.

1949	June 25. Nectar, Bowfell Neckband	K. Heaton. J. Umpleby. J. A. Jackson.
1949	June 25. Route 1, Right-hand Wall, Bowfell Neckband	K. Heaton. J. Umpleby. J. A. Jackson.
1949	June 26. Stewpot, Raven Crag	A. Gregory. A. R. Dolphin.
1949	June 27. Heather Slab, Tarn Crag.	J. W. Cook.
1949	July 3. Rib and Wall, Tarn Crag	A. Gregory. J. Woods.
1949	July 3. Orchid, Tarn Crag	A. Gregory. J. Woods. J. Renwick.
1949	July 3. Blandish, Tarn Crag	A. Gregory. J. Woods. J. Renwick.
1949	Aug. 28. West Buttress, Tarn Crag.	A. Gregory. J. Woods.
1949	Sept. 4. Gimmer Girdle	A. R. Dolphin. J. W. Cook.

The outcome of much wandering. On the 5th of July a complete traverse of the Crag had been achieved by J. W. Cook, J. G. Ball and L. J. Griffin, following an easier, and inferior, line across the N.W. face via Barry's Traverse and what was to become the second pitch of Godiva Groove.

1949 Sept. 7. Neckband Girdle   K. Heaton.
                                   S. Vernon.

1949 Sept. 18. Russet Groove,   A. R. Dolphin.
         White Ghyll   K. Heaton.
                    Alternate leads.

1949 Sept. 18. Inferno, White   K. Heaton.
         Ghyll   A. R. Dolphin.
                    Alternate leads.

1949 Oct. 8. The Gizzard,   K. Heaton.
         Bowfell Neckband   A. Heaton.

1950 Jan. 7. Godiva Groove,   C. M. G. Smith.
         Gimmer Crag   L. J. Griffin.

1950 June 11. Girdle Traverse,   A. R. Dolphin.
         Pavey Ark   J. B. Lockwood.
      4th June, 1950. Traverse as far as Jack's Rake. A. R. Dolphin,
      H. Schofield and A. D. Brown.

APPENDIX I

PAVEY ARK

GIRDLE TRAVERSE, PAVEY ARK.—725 feet. Very severe. A route of considerable interest and difficulty, steep rock pitches being interspersed with more vegetatious sections which present peculiar problems of their own. The crag is traversed from right to left from Hobson's Choice to Crescent Climb.

(1) 50 feet. From halfway up the gully a diagonal ascent is made to the left to ash-tree belay. (Pitch 1, Hobson's Choice.)

(2) 50 feet. Climb up to the grass shelf above the tree and follow it down to the left to a stance and small belay on the edge of a steep wall.

(3) 50 feet. A small holly-tree in the middle of the wall is the first objective—as a running belay. The traverse is then continued past the tree until an ascent can be made to a tiny ledge and raven's nest. Small belays, for sitting position, only.

(4) 25 feet. Move left over juniper to the foot of an open, grassy chimney which is climbed to stance and belay.

(5) 45 feet. Step round to the left and cross a steep, open scoop to a spike for running belay. Then descend obliquely left to a narrow grass ledge. Belay.

(6) 30 feet. Traverse easily left to the top of a groove. Belay.

(7) 50 feet. Descend the groove until an awkward stride can be made onto the vertical left wall, then straight up for a few feet to an awkward grassy mantelshelf (spike on the left for running belay). A very awkward

move round the overhanging corner on the left is
then made, followed by a short ascent to the large
shelf at the top of Pitch 4, Rake End Chimney.

(8)   20 feet.   Descend Pitch 4, Rake End Chimney.

(9)   35 feet.   Traverse out past a large, movable block onto
the face on the left of the chimney.   A steep scoop is
entered and ascended to a tiny ledge and running
belay eight feet higher.   Traverse left along the ledge
for 10 feet to a stance and two small belays—suitable
for line, only.

(10) 25 feet.   Step down and cross a corner on small holds.
A withered tree is at first rather useful for maintaining
balance but then becomes an obstacle in the attainment of a good ledge.   Belay.

(11) 35 feet.   Abseil down a vegetatious chimney to Jack's
Rake.

(12) 30 feet.   Walk up Jack's Rake and round to the left to
the top of Deception.

(13) 45 feet.   Descend the slab for a few feet and traverse left
into the corner and down it to a ledge and belay.
(Pitch 4, Deception, reversed.)

(14) 40 feet.   Descend over grass ledges to a ledge level with
a large overhang on the left.   (Pitch 3, Deception,
reversed.)

(15) 45 feet.   Traverse left under the overhang on good holds
for about 30 feet.   A rather awkward ascent can then
be made to the ledge and holly-tree belay at the top
of Pitch 2, Alph.

(16) 40 feet.   Following Alph for about 25 feet make an
awkward step up to the left, traverse to a shallow
groove and ascend to a good flake for running belay.

After a further short ascent traverse left over grass to a belay in a corner on Wailing Wall.

(17) 50 feet.   Step down and traverse left on small holds below a bulge until it is possible to step up onto a small ledge above the bulge.   Continue the traverse left round a steep corner to a large platform and belays.

(18) 60 feet.   Fairly easy climbing leftwards to Crescent Climb.

(19) Finish up, or down, Crescent Climb.

———

APPENDIX II

MOUNTAIN RESCUE

(Issued by the Mountain Rescue Committee, 1950)

FIRST AID POSTS AND EVACUATION ROUTES

Dungeon Ghyll Old Hotel, Great Langdale   *Tel : Grasmere* 72

Supervisor :   S. H. Cross (at the Old Hotel)

Doctors :   Dr. G. L. Lancaster.   Tel : Ambleside 388.
                 Dr. E. L. Fothergill.   Tel : Ambleside 170.
                 Dr. W. H. Mylechreest.   Tel : Ambleside 2.
                 Dr. A. F. Quarmby.   Tel : Ambleside 26.

Ambulance : Police Station, Ambleside.   Tel : 18.

Police :   Police Station, Langdale.   Tel. : Grasmere 39.
                 (Half-a-mile east of Elterwater on Ambleside Road).

Hospitals :   Kendal Hospital.   Tel : Kendal 71.
                 Manchester Royal Infirmary.   Tel : Ardwick 1721.
                 Leeds General Infirmary.   Tel : Leeds 20455.
                 Liverpool Royal Infirmary.   Tel : Royal 1900.

N.B.—After an accident please report to the Hon. Secretary, A. S. PIGOTT, Hill House, Cheadle Hulme, Stockport (Tel : Cheadle Hulme 257), giving particulars of equipment used and any deficiencies, as well as patient's name and address.

INDEX TO THE CLIMBS